PHILOSOPHICAL LEADERSHIP

BARBARA ASIMAKOPOULOU

An incredible source of leadership

Marshall Goldsmith
Thinkers 50 #1 Executive Coach,
#1 Leadership Thinker in the world,
New York Times bestselling author.

PHILOSOPHICAL LEADERSHIP

Become a better Leader through the lens of classical philosophy and coaching.

BY THE AWARD-WINNING INTERNATIONAL COACH
BARBARA ASIMAKOPOULOU

The present work is protected under the provisions of the Greek law 2112/1993 and international intellectual property conventions.

No part of this publication may be reproduced, adapted, stored in, or introduced into a retrieval system, or transmitted, in any form, or by any means (electronic, mechanical, photocopying, recording or otherwise), without the prior written permission of the publisher in accordance with Law 2121/1993 and the Berne International Convention (ratified by Law 100/1975).

Published in ...... 2023, in English
Author: Barbara Asimakopoulou
Title: Philosophical Leadership: Become a better Leader through the lens of classical philosophy and coaching
Cover Image by Darva Photography

Print: 978-1-76124-127-7
E-book: 978-1-76124-129-1
Hardback: 978-1-76124-128-4

Copyright © 2023 Barbara Asimakopoulou for the English language and all other languages

11, Olympionikon Sreet, Kryoneri, Athens, 145 68 Greece
Tel: +30 210 8160255
Email: ba@hre.gr
URL: www.barbaraasimakopoulou.com

First Published in 2018 under the title "Inner Emancipation" Coaching, Leadership & Philosophy by HRE, in Greek

Second Published in 2021 under the title "Inner Emancipation" Coaching, Leadership & Philosophy by HRE, in Greek

Publishing information
Publishing and design facilitated by Passionpreneur Publishing
A division of Passionpreneur Organization Pty Ltd
ABN: 48640637529

Melbourne, VIC | Australia
www.PassionpreneurPublishing.com

PRAISE FOR PHILOSOPHICAL COACHING

An incredible source of leadership by Barbara Asimakopoulou! Become an effective and ethical leader who achieves goals and lead your team to high performance with *Inner Emancipation*.

— **Marshall Goldsmith**
Thinkers 50 #1 Executive Coach and #1 Leadership Thinker in the world, the New York Times #1 bestselling author of Triggers, Mojo, and What Got You Here Won't Get You There

It ends up there is something new under the sun. Barbara Asimakopoulou explores the deepest roots of coaching, embedded in the philosophies of Socrates, Plato, and Aristotle. This is much more than a typical book on coaching or leadership. You will learn how to set yourself free!

— **Dave Wondra**
President, Wondra Group, LLC. Inducted into the International Coaching Federation Circle of Distinction

Profound, provocative, deep, and engaging – with an individual charm and a unique perspective. Barbara imbues her work with deep insights and wisdom reflecting on philosophy, leadership and coaching, to offer new and valuable perspectives. A must read and an excellent addition to your inspirational resources.

— **Kathryn Pope**
ICF PCC, Executive Coach, Team Coach,
Coach Supervisor, Resilience Coach

An excellent book on leadership. You make use of a wide variety of factors—ideas, spiritual elements, mental attributes, etc.—that indeed shape and characterise the leader. Frequent reference to Socrates adds another dimension to your book. Congratulations.

— **Georgios Babiniotis**
Professor at University of Athens,
Chairman of the Educational Society of Athens

I gained powerful life lessons, valuable instructions, food for thought, introspection, and reflection. Inner emancipation is the power to bring out our hidden potential and the liberation of our highest self from internal obstacles to achieve our most creative expression and development. Barbara shows us the way, drawing from three fields of knowledge—philosophy, leadership theory, and coaching—masterfully combining truths, lessons, and theories that lead to the desired goal.

Each page offers unique value. Philosophical quotes, leadership theories, practical advice from the field of coaching. It is not a book you put aside after reading it but a reference book you often consult to draw strength, inspiration, and knowledge.

I have known Barbara for years, and I consider her a living example of optimism, truth seeking, and willingness to help those around her using the valuable knowledge she has gained from thorough research and rich professional experience. I wish her wholeheartedly the best and to keep inspiring us with her work and living example. I also wish this book to become a valuable aid and guide for all of us on the path to inner emancipation.

— **Nancy Papalexandri**
Emeritus Professor HRM Athens University of Economics and Business

The question of what makes a good leader and how one can be developed has been incessantly debated since Plato's time. Relying on modern psychological theories and, most importantly, on Ancient Greek philosophy, Barbara Asimakopoulou proposes coaching as the best leadership development approach. The search for authenticity, self-knowledge, truth, freedom, and responsibility shapes a personality that refuses to be trapped in conventions and constantly seeks inner emancipation. The goal is the Aristotelian "eudaimonia."

Leaders who take inner emancipation seriously become catalysts for positive change, not only for themselves but also for others. This applies not only to those at the top of the pyramid but to anyone who has influence over other people—in short, all of us. Barbara Asimakopoulou maps the way to inner emancipation using simple, lucid, and up-to-date language. She popularises complex theories and philosophical ideas, incorporating them into modern management. Readers learn and are prompted to reflect. Business executives, in particular, have a lot to gain.

— **Haridimos Tsoukas**
Professor of Strategic Management at Columbia Ship Management, University of Cyprus, & Professor of Organisational Behaviour, University of Warwick

Ancient philosophy meets the principles of modern coaching and leadership, revealing our hidden possibilities and potential. The book is a great guide for this path.

— Antonia Katsoulieri
Editor-in-Chief HR Professional, Boussias Communications

Barbara Asimakopoulou's book was a very enjoyable experience, a precious gift to myself! I read it in one sitting, I really devoured it, and when I got to the end, I felt both wiser and stronger. Drawing on Ancient Greek philosophy, this book shows, in a masterful way, how to enrich your life (wellbeing) and fulfil your dreams, applying the Socratic self-knowledge (know thyself), tapping into your inner potential, and practicing the values of leadership according to Aristotelian ethics and logic.

A book with clear writing, combining scientific knowledge with modern coaching practices, that can become a tool for internal revolution and social well-being. Barbara Asimakopoulou, a top coach herself, generously shares her knowledge and experience on how to achieve our inner emancipation!

— Dr. Anna Karamanou
Former Chairman of the FEMM Committee of the European Parliament

Barbara Asimakopoulou sets forth an anthropocentric and holistic leadership, shedding light on ancient philosophical concepts and essential elements of modern coaching, management, and leadership. She demonstrates with clarity how important it is to realise our personal truth, and how beneficial it is to motivate and be motivated.

Philosophical Coaching is a thought-provoking book with a lot of useful tools for turning thoughts into action!

— **Evgenia Gkegkiou**
Chief People Officer at Viva Wallet

I read it almost in one sitting! Excellent flow and chapter analysis with many references to ancient philosophical texts. Clear, concise, and unpretentious writing illustrating the virtues of a good teacher. By introducing the term "inner emancipation," Barbara effectively describes the essence of coaching. Drawing from philosophy, she enriches the art and science of coaching by adding the imperative of self-knowledge, a concept often overlooked. Her optimistic statement that "we are all potential leaders" sends a strong message, expanding the concept of both participants and destination of the path, discarding the nowadays prevalent assumption that developing leadership skills requires individuals in need of guidance.

Overall, this book is a source of knowledge on the meaning of coaching. By connecting coaching with philosophy, Barbara follows the example of ancient philosophers. For them, the search for truth superseded the limitations of tradition. Similarly, this book succeeds to free coaching from "dogmas" and reach the coveted inner emancipation!

— **Cosmas Michael**
ICF Professional Certified Coach | Business Consulting | Coaching

Concepts such as leadership, self-leadership, Coach Leader, values, and timeless virtues take on another dimension in Barbara's book. They shape and shield human nature, conceptualise standards of professional behaviour, and give substance to all those things that lead to self-actualisation and self-fulfilment. This book could be viewed as an alternative approach to the dominant concepts that all professional coaches need to understand, explore, and above all, adopt—first for themselves and their own experiential path, but also for their clients and the improvement of their technique.

Everything I have studied in the past to gain awareness and improve my practice as a professional coach, I found in this book.

In addition, the author—as an experienced coach and HRM practitioner herself—explores how the art and science of coaching inspires people and shapes attitudes, behaviours, and cultures that develop individuals and relationships.

In simple but also scientific terms, the conceptual connection between Ancient Greek philosophy and modern coaching principles becomes clear as a dynamic framework for self-leadership, responsibility, achievement, and excellence. This book is highly recommended and is particularly relevant to those who consider the development of principles, framework, and harmony of vital importance.

— **Irene N. Nikolaidou**
Moving Minds Mng Partner | Professional Certified Executive & Team Coach by ICF | Certified mBIT Coach | Mentor Coach & Coach Supervisor | HRM Change Strategist

This book is definitely not the kind you read just once. This is a book that draws you in and won't let go. It is a friend and companion. You

PRAISE FOR PHILOSOPHICAL COACHING

constantly come back to discover a new point you identify with, a new aspect of your good self, a new opportunity for better, more meaningful communication with a partner or even a relative.

This book guides you to wisely manage the power you have if you are in a position of influence.

It guides you to encourage those who want to make their dreams come true.

It reminds you how important it is to constantly learn new things and not be afraid to approach differently what you did in a certain way until yesterday.

It reminds you to celebrate your successes.

It reminds you to welcome the constant changes in life and embrace them with humility and gratitude.

Barbara writes down her soul; she teaches with magnanimity and generosity and is the first one to apply what she captures in her books.

— **Lydia Antoniou**
Founder & CEO Lydia's Pastries

In a world that has lost its balance and purpose, Barbara's book comes to remind us of the meaning and purpose of life.

In a simple and practical way, it shows us that only by turning inwards can we identify what is important and that leadership always unfolds from the inside out.

Ancient Greek philosophy combined with coaching becomes a compass and equips coaches with the necessary knowledge and tools to achieve their goals, understand the bigger picture, and become the best version of themselves.

— Olga Papatriantafyllou
Founder of Mindfulness Institute | M.B.S.R teacher | Coach | Psychotherapist

To my beloved community of V.I.P.
Visionary, **I**nnovative, & **P**owerful
Coaches and Leaders

TABLE OF CONTENTS

Praise for Philosophical Coaching	v
Acknowledgments	xix
Introduction	1
Purpose	5
Aim	7
Structure	9
Preface	13

STEP 1
COACHING AND ITS BENEFITS 21

STEP 2
CLASSICAL PHILOSOPHY AND COACHING 37

STEP 3
THE PATH TO A NEW LEADER PROFILE 69

Step 4
THE COACH LEADER 97

STEP 5
THE FUNDAMENTAL SKILLS OF THE COACH LEADER 121

STEP 6
COACHING LEADERSHIP: VALUES-BASED LEADERSHIP 149

STEP 7
PHILOSOPHERSHIP™:
THE PHILOSOPHICAL MODEL OF LEADERSHIP 169

STEP 8
FIRST-TIME LEADER 189

Afterword 205
Recommended bibliography 207
About the author 213
Personal letter 217

The only one who can save humanity, or destroy it, are humans themselves, and especially those in positions of influence: the leaders. Therefore, every individual is a potential leader because they consciously or unconsciously influence every person close to them. Undoubtedly, the first person they influence is themselves.

ACKNOWLEDGMENTS

I am thankful to all the people in my life who support, uplift, and inspire me.

A very special thanks to:

All my "teachers," to whom I refer by name in this book.

The academic board, the faculty, my students and graduates at "Coaching Skills and Tools in Practice," my hybrid Coaching Education Program with accreditation from the leading professional body, the International Coaching Federation (who "endorsed" with their participation and enthusiasm the approach and ideas you will find in this book), and those at "Coaching Leadership: In the Footsteps of Socrates," the e-learning program I have designed and have the honour to implement for the National Kapodistrian University of Athens, Greece.

My beloved clients—both individuals and corporations—whose unique examples and stories enrich my life and shape my bigger purpose.

My family. My beloved partner in life and work; my two amazing sons, who are my beacon of light and source of energy; my father, who makes me stronger by his example; my mother, who makes me braver with her overwhelming love and faith in me.

The distinguished people, professionals, friends, colleagues, associates, and partners who offered their feedback with touching eagerness.

All of you, who hold this book in your hands and embark on the wonderful adventure of "**Philosophical Leadership**" for a "full" life.

"Future development depends on people's emancipation."

— ALEC ROSS, *INDUSTRIES OF THE FUTURE*,
ATHENS: IKAROS

INTRODUCTION

If my life had been a book and the last decade a chapter within it, the book would be titled: *An Unstoppable Warrior Under Tense Creativity.* However, at the dawn of a new critical decade in my life, I needed to close the previous chapter and open a new one—a new me—"*A Peaceful and Wise Leader and Entrepreneur.*"

The global economic crisis deeply affected me, personally and professionally. The implications of the crisis for Greece were profound. However, these years coincided with the most creative and hectic time of my career and my painstaking personal and professional maturity.

I call this time "**the path to my inner emancipation**."

The inspiration to write this book has been in me for years and was slowly fertilised by my restless interest in self-actualisation and achievement.

Fortunately, **coaching** came early as a *deus ex machina*, reinforcing my survival toolkit on this lonely but fascinating journey.

Then came **philosophy**, broadening my thinking and soothing my existential concerns.

My maturity went hand in hand with my ever-increasing desire to awaken society to holistically healthier businesses—businesses that ensure not only survival or progress but also satisfaction and happiness. I believe that the basis of an ethical and sustainable society is authentic and ethical people, liberated from internal limiting beliefs.

My biggest motivation for this book is to activate new leaders in this direction. *How?* In the same way I was triggered: **by following the rough but redemptive path of inner leadership through coaching and philosophy**.

Through the internal revolution of taking responsibility for yourself and your choices; the liberation from all sorts of untrue interpretations, limiting conventions and beliefs; the expression and practice of your true capabilities and desires; the enjoyment of the journey; genuine maturity.

Through the journey to your authentic self.

Through the unique and critical prerequisite before you lead others: **by leading yourself first**.

— Barbara Asimakopoulou

"Look to improve yourself for your own benefit and others will follow."

— ANTISTHENES 45-465 BC *FRAGMENTS,*
FRAGMENT 74

PURPOSE

In this book, I present the **Coach Leader**, an everyday leader who is always a coach, inspired by classic Greek philosophy.

The leadership style I propose transforms every person into an ethical and effective leader, first of themselves and then of others.

This book aims to provide an alternative approach to leadership for every current or future leader who wishes to control themselves and their decisions and attain inner emancipation (the original title of the edition in the Greek language).

AIM

This book addresses all those who strive for inner leadership and liberation from any constraint that obscures their authentic self and outer actions.

Everyone who wishes to practice leadership, first for themselves and then for others, and to achieve *eudaimonia*, a flourishing life.

Everyone who wishes to be a role model and facilitate the development of people in their personal or professional journey.

Current and future leaders, new or experienced business executives, entrepreneurs, and professionals who want to incorporate philosophy and coaching into their leadership style.

More specifically:

- those who want to be themselves, achieve their goals, and enjoy the journey
- those who want to lead their team to high performance and maintain a peaceful and creative work environment

- those who wish to have dedicated and competent partners
- those who want to coach exceptional people that will stand out and lead their team to victory under any circumstances.

STRUCTURE

This book consists of eight chapters, each of which describes a step toward inner and outer leadership and collective well-being, as follows:

STEP 1: COACHING AND ITS BENEFITS

This chapter details the methodology and value of the modern art and science of coaching, especially its crucial role in shaping the personality of the Coach Leader, with its distinctive qualities and skills.

STEP 2: CLASSICAL PHILOSOPHY AND COACHING

This chapter offers a comparison of Ancient Greek philosophy with the principles and practice of modern coaching. Coaching is closely related to the teachings of Socrates, Plato, and Aristotle. This step reinforces coaching as a lifestyle for the Coach Leader with outstanding benefits.

STEP 3: THE PATH TO A NEW LEADER PROFILE

Modern conditions pave the way for the everyday leader seeking inner leadership through self-knowledge, self-responsibility, and their influence on their environment. Ancient Greek virtues, along with values, reinforce and guide the behaviour of the Coach Leader, as described in this chapter.

STEP 4: THE COACH LEADER

The Coach Leader envisions an ethical, sustainable society with happy people. In this chapter, the characteristics of a modern ideal leader are compared with those of a professional coach. A synthesis of the Coach Leader's characteristics and everyday leadership is presented.

STEP 5: THE FUNDAMENTAL SKILLS OF THE COACH LEADER

The most important skills of the Coach Leader, such as trust building, active listening, the art of speech, the art of effective questioning, vision co-creation, acknowledgement, creative conflict resolution, and effective communication, are described in this chapter.

STEP 6: COACHING LEADERSHIP: VALUES-BASED LEADERSHIP

This chapter presents the Coach Leader in action, leading and energising people by uncovering their most important values. Coach Leaders identify their own values, then those of the people they influence. Furthermore, they create a shared motivational vision that includes these values.

STEP 7: PHILOSOPHERSHIP™: THE PHILOSOPHICAL MODEL OF LEADERSHIP

This chapter illustrates the original leadership and strategy model of the Coach Leader. This model brings philosophy, existential reflection, and coaching together for the first time as part of a leadership model. The effectiveness of this model is based on people's commitment to a higher purpose, which they create with the help of the Coach Leader.

STEP 8: FIRST-TIME LEADER AND COACHING

Coach Leaders who take on this role for the first time lead their team to victory by shifting the focus from personal ambition to effective team management. Coach Leaders guarantee successful teams and happy people, as explored in this chapter.

PREFACE

People's growth and development depend on many factors, but mainly on their attitude towards external or internal obstacles and their commitment to their goals. Similarly, the growth of a business or an organisation can be attained through committed individuals working together toward a common goal.

The leader is a catalyst throughout this process.

LEADERSHIP

According to leading academic researchers, global thinkers, intellectuals, and successful professionals, every person who has influence is considered a leader, especially those with official positions of influence and responsibility. According to the distinguished Greek linguist and university professor Georgios Babiniotis, the word "influence" refers to a form of power and, more generally, the impact exerted on specific individuals (*Dictionary of Synonyms and Antonyms*, p. 433).

Every individual, professional, entrepreneur, executive—**all of us—exert influence** on one or more people, consciously or unconsciously. Thus, **we are all potential leaders**.

I believe that **the greater the number of people influenced by a leader, the greater the responsibility**. It is evident that this is a demanding task requiring support and assistance, as is the case with any challenging project.

In the case of leadership, we need help to understand and manage the issues that affect our behaviour and that of the people in our sphere of influence. Therefore, all active or potential leaders need:

- to have self-knowledge, to be able to recognise the motives that drive their behaviour and how they influence their decisions and effectiveness
- to assume responsibility for their choices and decisions
- to overcome internal and external obstacles or restrictive beliefs that hinder their path to inner emancipation and bold decision making
- to recognise the motivations that guide people's behaviour and influence their decisions and performance
- to better understand human relationships to improve and enjoy their collaborations
- to inspire and support people to find solutions to their problems
- to create a shared vision toward a prosperous and sustainable society
- to develop authentic and emancipated successor leaders.

PREFACE

PHILOSOPHY, COACHING, AND LEADERSHIP

Many different theories on effective leadership have been created, analysed, and adopted.

In this book, I present the **Coach Leader**, a modern-day leader who guarantees social change toward an ethical and sustainable society.

Coach Leaders combine philosophy with coaching and apply this knowledge in their personal and professional lives. The basic foundations are **self-knowledge** and **ongoing evolution** for individual and collective well-being.

We all can, and therefore have a responsibility to, positively influence the people close to us—every small or large group in our sphere of influence.

THE FREEDOM OF CHOICE

Aristotle argues that to enjoy a happy life, one must possess the curiosity of a scientist and the existential pursuit of a philosopher, make time for enjoyment every day, and simultaneously be a responsible and active citizen. In a broader sense, we should recognise that we all have the freedom of choice to live according to the above. This freedom of choice makes us responsible and accountable, first and foremost, to ourselves.

Self-accountability is the quintessential capability of a mature individual and is linked to the assertion of freedom of choice.

To conclude, when a person decides **to influence** their immediate environment positively and consciously, we have the model of **a leader**. When we add **coaching** to this choice, we have the **Coach Leader**, who unleashes people's potential, cares about them holistically, and prepares successor leaders.

In order to galvanise the Coach Leader, I created the **Philosophership™** model, inspired by classic Greek philosophy.

The great masters of Greek antiquity have explored all these issues, and so well that it would be a tragic indifference and blasphemy to disregard them in our daily lives as modern Greeks.

Lately, Ancient Greek values and ideas have gained currency internationally, especially in the US. Professor Martin Seligman, the father of positive psychology, cites Aristotle's virtues as a prerequisite for a happy life. Modern Stoicism revives the teaching of Epictetus. The more I delve into Ancient Greek philosophy, the more amazed I am at the valuable life lessons that are still relevant today.

The value of these life lessons becomes ever more evident at a time when the global community is seeking solutions toward a more ethical, fair, and sustainable society.

I firmly believe that the Coach Leader is the solution, and I refer to Ancient Greek philosophy because it is part of my national history, my DNA. Those who forget their past are doomed to repeat it.

Why repeat the mistakes of the past when we are fortunate enough to have this enviable legacy?

What is incomprehensible is practically non-existent. I am sure none of the philosophers mentioned in this book would want to stay "non-existent" or forgotten on a dusty shelf, even if their teaching is not entirely conveyed. I feel like I am bringing them back to life, all while gaining new life myself!

I hope you will soak up this energy, as my students and I do during the program I designed for the National Kapodistrian University of Athens, "Coaching Leadership: In the Footsteps of Socrates," where I first introduced the Coach Leader and the Philoshophership™ model.

> My aspiration is to revive all the treasures of Ancient Greek thought on how to live a meaningful life and, with great respect to their gravitas, bring them closer to everyday life.

I invite you to follow the next eight steps.

Each step brings you closer to inner leadership and transforms you into a leader, first of yourself and then of others. These steps require only a **good disposition and perseverance** on your part.

EIGHT STEPS
TOWARD INNER AND OUTER LEADERSHIP, PERSONAL AND SOCIAL WELLBEING

STEP 1

COACHING AND ITS BENEFITS

"Coaching is a holistic approach to human development. It has to do with the ability to feel, think, and enjoy."

— BARBARA ASIMAKOPOULOU

PURPOSE

In this first step, I invite you to recognise the value of the modern art and science of coaching in shaping the Coach Leader's personality and leadership skills.

1.1. The definition of coaching

Coaching is the revival of the **Socratic method** regarding the search for truth. It combines the teachings of Socrates, Aristotle, and other classic Greek philosophers with the modern sciences of psychology—especially Positive Psychology—neuroscience, philosophy, anthropology, biology, sociology, business, and management, aiming at human development.

The International Coaching Federation (ICF) gives the clearest and most comprehensive definition of coaching.

The ICF defines coaching as partnering with clients in a thought-provoking and creative process that inspires them to maximise their personal and professional potential.

A professional coach, according to the ICF:

- practices the eight ICF Core Competencies
- adheres to and is accountable under the ICF Code of Ethics.

The **eight core competencies** and **code of ethics** set out the proper coaching process and the appropriate framework of professional conduct to ensure effectiveness, enhance the credibility and validity of each professional coach, and protect the client.

International Coaching Federation

Founded in 1995, the ICF is dedicated to advancing the coaching profession by setting high standards, providing independent certification, and building a worldwide network of credentialed coaches. ICF is a global organisation with a membership comprising more than 50,000 professional personal and business coaches located in over 150 countries and territories.

The ICF continues to offer the most globally recognised, independent credentialing program for coach practitioners. ICF credentials are awarded to professional coaches who have met stringent education and experience requirements and have demonstrated a thorough understanding of the coaching competencies that set the standard in the profession. Achieving credentials through ICF signifies a coach's commitment to integrity, understanding and mastery of coaching skills, and dedication to clients.

The ICF also accredits programs that deliver coaching education. ICF-accredited education organisations must complete a rigorous review process and demonstrate that their curriculum aligns with the ICF Core Competencies and Code of Ethics. The professional credentials ensuring the competence and integrity of the coach are the following: **ACC** (Associate Certified Coach)—first level, **PCC** (Professional Certified Coach)—second level, and **MCC** (Master Certified Coach)—third and highest level.

Professional certification ensures that the practitioner has been adequately trained, evaluated, supervised by a Mentor Coach, and tested in writing on the eight core competencies, the code of ethics, and their understanding of key definitions.

All ICF professionals need to possess and systematically demonstrate knowledge of the eight core competencies and are required to adhere to the code of ethics in order to maintain and renew their credentials and to ensure that they offer services of the highest quality to their clients.

The art and science of coaching

Below are more insights to help you understand the art and science of coaching.

The process

Coaching is not just a theoretical tool or methodology. It is a specific practical process with a beginning, middle, and end.

During this process, the coach facilitates and motivates the coachee to set personal or professional goals and to achieve them by resolving internal (personal) and external (practical) barriers, having first applied the same process on themselves.

Coaching supports the holistic development of every person

Coaches explore the thoughts, emotions, and desires of the coachees, addressing the three radars of their existence: **mind**, **heart**, and **soul**. In particular, they possess the ability to think for themselves and their environment, the ability to feel the effects of their actions, and ultimately, the ability to enjoy success and life in general.

According to **Plato** (Republic), the soul is divided into three parts: *logos* (reason), *pathos* (emotions), and *eros* (desire). Logos is the mind and the perception of our environment and our actions, pathos refers to our heart and emotions, and eros is the motivation that drives our behaviour.

Modern management gurus like Dr. Daniel Goleman, professor at Harvard University and author of the international bestseller *Working with Emotional Intelligence*, argue that pathos (emotions) clearly influences human outcomes. Indeed, Goleman calls this the **Emotional Intelligence or Quotient**.

Specifically, the Emotional Quotient (emotions—heart) contrasts with the **Intelligence Quotient** (reason—brain).

According to **Howard Gardner**, an American researcher, professor of medicine and neurology at Boston University School of Medicine, and predecessor of Goleman, there are **nine types of intelligence** (*Frames of Mind: The Theory of Multiple Intelligences*).

One of these is existential intelligence. Dimitris Bourantas, Professor at the Athens University of Economics and Business, eloquently refers to social, political, and existential intelligence (in his books *On Stage Without Rehearsal* and *Leadership Meta-Competencies: Discovering Hidden Virtues*).

In my opinion, **all three of these intelligences concern eros (desire)**, the third part of the soul, according to Plato. They explain the "why" and "how" behind a person's motivation and behaviour.

The role of coaching is to help the coachees understand the functioning and interdependence of the three parts of the soul (reason, emotions, and desires) to help them adopt the appropriate behaviours and achieve their goals.

Coaching aims at the overall satisfaction of the coachee in all important areas of their life, such as personal development, home, family, friends, social life, romantic love, work, financial resources, health, leisure, spirituality, and social contribution.

Coaching has emerged—and continues to emerge—as a prominent trend in leadership development and team leadership. It increases the effectiveness of both the leader and the team by empowering people at a personal and group level, revealing hidden potential.

> Coaching, like classic Greek philosophy, is human-centred.

1.2. The core of coaching success

Below, I explain the reason why coaching is a powerful process that leads to successful leadership, first of ourselves and then of others.

The key to coaching success

Coaches are trained to facilitate each person's discovery of the most appropriate solutions for themselves.

They succeed because they dig and reveal each person's true desires (I want) and capabilities (I can) and then support them to find the best solutions for themselves.

> Coaches believe that clients hold the key to solving every problem they face.
>
> Only the client can give the best solution.

This is true because only the coachees have access to all the details of the problem. With the help of the coach, they bring these details to the surface and discover the solution.

Finding the solution themselves ensures that the action plan is relevant to their true capabilities, knowledge, and aspirations, and it guarantees greater commitment and dedication to the goal.

Thus, bringing every aspect of the problem to the surface and allowing the coachees to find the most appropriate solution ensures their commitment to the necessary actions and increases the likelihood of a successful outcome.

1.3. The father of modern coaching

Thomas J. Leonard

Thomas Leonard is considered by many to be the father of modern business and life coaching.

In 1992, he founded Coach U (Coach University), the International Association of Coaches (IAC), and CoachVille (coaching and training network); in 1995, he founded the International Coaching Federation (ICF).

He has written six books on coaching, along with 14 internally published works, available exclusively to Coach University coaches. In 1998, he launched TeleClass.com, a virtual university with more than 20,000 students, offering over 100 teleclasses per week delivered via video conferencing. He has designed 28 personal and professional development programs used by coaches, training companies, and Fortune 100 companies.

Thomas Leonard is considered a visionary and a masterful composer of ideas. Sadly, he passed away at the height of his creativity and career.

"A lifestyle is what you pay for; a life is what pays you."
"Integrity reveals beauty."

— THOMAS LEONARD, EXECUTIVE COACH (1955–2003)

1.4. Socrates—the first coach

Socrates

Image: From Sting, CC BY-SA 2.5, https://commons.wikimedia.org/w/index.php?curid=3569936.

The famous dialectic method of Socrates and his faith in human beings and the truth that lies within them are at the core of the art, science, and practice of modern coaching. For this reason, Greek coaches, as well as coaches worldwide, argue that Socrates was, in fact, the first coach.

Coaches challenge, inspire, and ultimately provide the best outlet for each individual and all of us collectively, with a future-oriented attitude. It is my personal belief, and it has been proven in practice, that this is achieved through the values of integrity, ethics, and wisdom that are at the heart of Ancient Greek philosophy and also form part of the ICF Code of Ethics. All coaches trained and certified through ICF pledge to abide by the code of ethics in order to claim and maintain their ICF credentials and to ensure their professional credibility.

In **the second step**, we will examine in detail the relationship between coaching and the teaching of Socrates and other philosophers.

> *"I do not know or teach anything; I have only questions."*
> — SOCRATES (470–399 BC) PLATO, *SOCRATES' APOLOGY*[1]

---

[1] The concept is expressed in Socrates' defense during his trial. In the "Apology," Socrates states that the Oracle of Delphi declared him the wisest of all men because he was aware of his own ignorance.

1.5. Invest in yourself

Investing in coaching means investing in yourself. It is one of the most important actions you can take, but it is also the most neglected one.

Coaching is the best investment one can make today to achieve clarity and personal and professional growth.

Coaches support every person that has difficulties in finding motivation to set clear goals and achieve them. They help coachees identify and resolve internal or external barriers that prevent them from growing. They patiently and carefully support them to make the **best decisions for themselves**.

Coaching can help you:

- discover your creative, better self
- increase confidence and self-awareness
- overcome potential fears that stifle you
- consistently follow the appropriate action plan to achieve your goals
- take advantage of every new opportunity presented
- maintain the balance between work and personal life.

1.6. Coaching as a catalyst for change

Coaching in Greece, judging by the exponential growth shown in recent years with the pivotal help of the Greek ICF chapter, **unlocks**

more and more Greeks, as Socrates did 2500 years ago when exploring the unique truth hidden within each individual.

The greatest value that coaching has to offer to people, whether individuals or business and social groups, is *change*. If a person, a group, a business, or a society in general needs a change of culture or a change in mass behaviour, coaching is the best method.

In order to change, people need:

- to discover the benefit, what is best for them
- to treat obstacles as a problem to be resolved, not as an excuse to abandon the effort.

In a nutshell, people need spiritual and emotional commitment in order to be mobilised and overcome obstacles.

Logic alone is not enough—they also need to commit emotionally.

> Coaching increases the intellectual and emotional commitment of people. It changes their way of thinking and ensures behavioural change.

Emotional commitment comes when there is soul behind every desire. That is, motivation, the "eros" part of the soul.

We will now examine how change is achieved, how a new behaviour is established, and how a new culture is formed (attitudes, beliefs, behaviours).

Creating a new culture

The first step in creating a new culture is raising awareness on the importance of that change. This way, people are prepared to accept it and overcome any potential obstacles.

> An old habit can only be replaced by a new one.

The most critical step is to **practice the new behaviour consistently and systematically**. With practice, the new behaviour will begin to manifest automatically. **Culture is something that happens automatically** as part of ourselves, our routine, our daily life; it does not require any prior spiritual or emotional processing.

For people to maintain a certain behaviour consistently and systematically, they need a reminder. Self-commitment is very difficult. The more a behaviour is repeated, the stronger the commitment.

The coach reminds you of any new beneficial behaviour and supports you throughout this new practice to overcome the obstacles that come your way, either by you (internally) or by third parties (externally).

How much practice does it take? One day, two days, three days?

A long-established culture cannot be erased overnight. It takes a lot of practice over an extended period of time. It may take one year, two years, three years.

> The coach is your alarm clock and your guardian angel for every dark part inside of you.

1.7. Executive coaching

Executive coaching is a process of professional support for employed or non-employed executives and professionals of all levels who are currently facing simple or complex problems.

This process gradually awakens the creative thinking of the supported executive and expands their personal and professional potential for future decisions.

Today more than ever, we need a scientific approach to decision making because we need alternative ways of thinking, innovative ideas, and most importantly, bold actions.

For this to be achieved, there needs to be a solid foundation, which is no other than the authentic "want" and "can" of every individual. The coach—be it life coach, executive coach, business coach, or health coach—always starts from the base of self-knowledge.

Groups of people that benefit from an executive coach include:

- anyone in a stage of transition or reinvention
- leaders at any hierarchical level or domain
- executives facing professional or personal challenges
- entrepreneurs and freelancers
- executives after a short or long absence from work
- teams that need to be energised and to communicate and perform better.

Let us examine the benefits for each group separately.

Executive coaching will enable leaders and executives facing challenges to:

- create new strategies for their company or organisation; develop teamwork; and ensure commitment to a common vision, value, or goal
- lead their team effectively
- achieve high and demanding goals after being promoted to managerial positions
- move forward in their careers and take full advantage of their potential and talents
- discover new career opportunities.

Executive coaching will enable teams to:

- be empowered and guided in times of crisis, mergers, and organisational or other changes
- be motivated for better and faster results
- be aligned with the vision, values, and goals of the company or organisation
- resolve conflicts and cooperate and communicate effectively.

Executive coaching will allow professionals and entrepreneurs to:

- start or grow their business, clarify their needs, prioritise, and take action
- make drastic changes
- share their vision, values, and goals
- resolve problems with their staff
- have less stress and more free time.

Executive coaching is also helpful for women who face personal and professional difficulties, such as starting a new career, being promoted, claiming a leadership position, or establishing a better work–life balance.

> Coaching supports you in discovering your true personal and professional desires and acting to achieve your goals. Coaching supports you to adopt the appropriate behaviour, be transformed, discover the opportunity behind each challenge, and finally live authentically in the pursuit of "eudaimonia."

POINTS TO REMEMBER FROM STEP 1

- To change a behaviour that does not serve my vision, I first need to achieve the following through coaching:
    - realise the value of the new behaviour
    - dedicate and engage myself spiritually and emotionally in the process of change
    - practice the new behaviour consistently for as long as it takes.
- Only a human-centric coach who understands the natural propensity for resistance to change can help you overcome intellectual and emotional resistance, mobilise you, and at the same time support you throughout this process.
- The biggest benefit a good professional coach can offer you is CHANGE.

PHILOSOPHICAL LEADERSHIP

YOUR TURN

Immediate action I will take:

Are there any obstacles? If so, what are they?

How will I overcome each obstacle?

STEP 2

CLASSICAL PHILOSOPHY AND COACHING

"Philosophy has developed over millennia to help us grapple with fundamental questions regarding the meaning of life and how to live a happy life. Coaching facilitates the whole process so that we can live with excellence and achieve eudaimonia."

— BARBARA ASIMAKOPOULOU

PURPOSE

The purpose of the second step is to shed light on the relationship between modern coaching and philosophy, from the times of Socrates, Plato, and Aristotle to the most representative figures of the modern world.

In this step, I attempt, with great attention and humility, to compare the principles and patterns of behaviour that stem from classic Ancient Greek philosophy with the principles and practice of modern coaching. I begin with Socrates and Aristotle, and then I attempt a convergence between these philosophies, summarising the main points.

The reason why I so enthusiastically compare the legacy of great philosophers with the modern art and science of coaching is that it will allow you to shape your personal Coach Leader profile with complete awareness and strength of spirit and soul so that you can stand out, acquire influence, and leave your mark.

Also, this insight will confirm that you have chosen the best path for your personal growth and the growth of the lucky team that has you as a leader today or will have you in the future!

Looking closely at the relevant sources, it is easy to see that positive psychology **resuscitates** Ancient Greek philosophy through a modern and thorough approach based on research and scientific validity.

We observe a general **revival of the Ancient Greek philosophical principles** regarding **human awakening** toward a better life. I dare to draw a comparison between the Italian Renaissance inspired by classical Greek art and philosophy and the modern revival of Ancient Greek philosophy through positive psychology and coaching, which began in the mid-1990s in America and then spread to Europe with the modern trend of Stoic philosophy at the University of Exeter in England.

The French historian Jules Michelet coined the term "renaissance," or "revival," to sum up the innovations of the 15th and 16th centuries, meaning "**the discovery of the world and the discovery of human**."

Humanism, the major intellectual movement of the Renaissance, from the era of Petrarch (1304–1374) onwards, was mainly focused on how man can live, combining ethical philosophy and the knowledge of classical antiquity.

Philosophy, during the transition period between the Middle Ages and the modern era, became more and more interested in people, history, and nature.

In my opinion, the **mid-90s revival of classical philosophy and classical principles such as self-knowledge, self-regulation, the golden mean, and the search for what makes a good life, a flourishing life**, was not a sudden occurrence.

The modern way of life, characterised by the ruthless pursuit of material goods and worldly power, has deprived people of the basic values and joys of human nature, such as selfless love, friendship, contact with nature, and self-fulfilment. With the help of modern scientists, philosophers, psychologists, sociologists, and (of course) coaches, the above imbalance came to the surface. In their effort to provide solutions to the impasses, these experts began employing **timeless philosophical questions** and, of course, the answers given in the past.

2.1. The legacy of classic Ancient Greece in coaching

Eudaimonia–excellence–wisdom

In the first subsection, I present the philosophical questions and the models of behaviour as bequeathed to us by the classic Greek philosophers.

Then, I compare them with the relevant theory and practice of modern coaching. My aim is to support and facilitate the Coach Leader in the exercise of everyday leadership.

2.1.1. What do philosophers explore?

A philosopher, according to the Ancient Greeks and the etymology of the word, is someone who loves wisdom and knowledge.

The philosopher is motivated by curiosity and love of knowledge and truth, but also by an internal compulsion to discover answers about WHY (the reason) we live and HOW (the way) we should live.

Philosophers throughout history have been exploring the reason behind human existence, the meaning of life, and how we should live to be happy. They have considered how to function in daily life, how to relate to others, and how to claim things, all while remaining true to our existence, deepest desires, and values. To achieve this goal, philosophers focus on the essence of reality and the human behaviour that results from it.

The Ancient Greek philosophers, fuelled by the love of knowledge, sought answers to the above existential issues. Their views appealed greatly to the Western world and laid the foundations of Western philosophy and psychology. They influenced modern philosophers, such as Russell, Kant, and Sartre, and modern psychologists, such as Maslow, Csikszentmihalyi, Seligman, May, and Yalom.

Most of the classical Ancient Greek views regarding the reason of existence and the appropriate way of living have not lost a drop of their credibility and remain a beacon of light to this day—especially now that the Western world is desperately looking for answers to a strong, more ethical restart!

2.1.2. Classic Ancient Greek philosophy and modern coaching

Here, I present some of the principles of classic Ancient Greek philosophy, starting with Socrates; at the same time, I offer a comparison with modern coaching principles.

Man is the centre of *everything*

Socrates was the first philosopher to explore human nature and the soul. As Cicero put it, Socrates was the first to call philosophy down from the heavens.

The main object of philosophy before Socrates was the investigation of natural phenomena. Socrates put people, their surroundings, and society at the centre of philosophical pursuits.

The coaching process

Just as philosophy has people at its centre and explores why and how he should live to achieve well-being, the science of coaching puts people at its centre to achieve the exact same purpose.

The search for truth

Socrates' main purpose in life was the search for truth—the one that people hide within themselves. He was searching for the "universal" truth. He was not satisfied with incomplete conclusions.

He begins all his dialogues with the principle that he knows nothing and tries to guide or provoke his interlocutors to reveal weaknesses in their own views or assumptions.

Through the art of dialogue and questioning, they arrive together at the truth—which, according to Socrates, exists from the beginning but is hidden. This is why it takes effort to discover it and bring it to light.

The process of seeking the truth through knowledge and its practice leads to the virtue of wisdom.

The coaching process

Coaching is the ultimate **process of seeking the truth that lies within each individual** regarding their views, ideas, feelings, desires, perceptions, and assumptions.

According to coaching, each person hides a unique truth.

Self-knowledge

Socrates considers self-knowledge a fundamental principle. He constantly urges the reader to "be a lamp unto yourself." As I have already mentioned, self-knowledge is an ongoing process acquired through reflection and experience.

The coaching process

Self-knowledge is the foundation and starting point of the coaching process.

"Know thyself."

The first of three Delphic maxims inscribed in the forecourt of the Temple of Apollo at Delphi attributed to one of the seven sages of the antiquity Thales of Miletus, Chilon of Sparta, Solon of Athens, Pittacus of Mytilene, Bias of Priene, Cleoboulos of Rhodes and Periander of Corinth.

The meaning of the phrase is discussed in Plato's Protagoras dialogue by Socrates

"I know that I know nothing."

— SOCRATES
PLATO, *SOCRATES' APOLOGY*[2]

The coach facilitates the process of finding, first and foremost, your true self and your authentic desires and talents.

---

[2] The concept is expressed in Socrates' defense during his trial. In the "Apology," Socrates states that the Oracle of Delphi declared him the wisest of all men because he was aware of his own ignorance.

The constant search for knowledge

Socrates asserts the infinity of human ignorance. He argues that people do not really know what they think they know.

Learning is a painful and endless journey. Socrates set the search for knowledge as his ultimate life goal, especially after the oracle of Delphi proclaimed him the wisest of the wise, an honour that he could not accept, deeply pious and humble as he was.

In order to "bear" this honorary oracle, he gave his own interpretation: the gods had chosen him as the wisest because of his admission of ignorance. So, he made it his life's purpose to prove it.

The coaching process

Coaching advocates that human behaviour is often indicated by assumptions that are fundamentally false. People often believe things about themselves that are not true and hinder their development.

In many cases, there is ignorance or misinterpretation of reality and views based on stereotypes or false assumptions.

Coaches, at the beginning of every coaching conversation, declare that it is the coachee who possesses the knowledge, not themselves.

The coachees are in the unique position of knowing what is best for them and what is the solution to their every problem.

The coach's responsibility is to uncover this authentic self-knowledge.

Coaches, especially if they have worked as consultants (e.g., I used to work as an HR consultant), are often impressed by the final choices the coachees make, and they constantly confirm that the coachee is always the expert.

Limitations and prejudices

Socrates sought to stimulate critical thinking in people, to reveal their limitations and to challenge the assumptions on which they built their lives and made their choices.

It was particularly disturbing to those who preferred to live in a fake but socially "safe" world. But Socrates never stopped arguing that the truth is the only path to human progress and happiness.

The coaching process

Coaching helps people discover their limitations and redefine them on a new, more realistic base. The coachees are challenged to discover wrong assumptions and prejudices that unjustly prevent their growth.

Challenging means politely contesting by asking the right questions

Socrates constantly asked questions, even embarrassing ones.

He believed that controversy is creative because it leads to truth and, ultimately, to the improvement of people.

The coaching process

The coach asks questions that often create embarrassment or confusion because they lead to discoveries and revelations.

The coach does not take anything for granted until the truth is revealed by the coachees themselves.

Seeing beyond the apparent

Socrates believed that philosophers need to see beyond the apparent, meaning beyond the senses, because the world is not at all as it seems. This is achieved through contemplation (similar to today's mindfulness).

In contemplation mode, the mind stops working on autopilot and starts to work beneficially toward people's awareness.

The coaching process

The coach tries to see beyond what the coachee says or does. They maintain an open mind, free from prejudice, and use the technique of reflection.

No one becomes evil of their own free will

According to Socrates, no one does evil knowing that it is evil.

We can all be good when we possess the highest virtue, knowledge, and specifically the knowledge of objective truth, meaning the judgment to distinguish good from evil.

The coaching process

In coaching, there is no good or bad coachee, no good or bad behaviour. The coachee is neither judged nor instructed.

The coach can help the coachee bring to light the objective truth, the unique truth of every human being, such as their talents or weaknesses.

Everyone is responsible for their own actions

With his death, Socrates taught us a valuable lesson: that every human being must assume responsibility for their own actions. He chose to remain true to his principles and was fully responsible for that choice.

The coaching process

The coach clarifies from the beginning that coachees are responsible for their actions and the consequences of these actions.

The coach supports their decisions wholeheartedly, without prejudice or judgment. The coachees should be fully aware of the consequences and assume responsibility for the outcomes.

2.2. The Socratic method

What was the Socratic method of teaching? How did he search for the truth? What patterns of behaviour did he cultivate? What example did he set?

All of the above are the basis of the coaching process.

The Socratic method—the revelation of truth

Socrates wanted to uncover the objective truth through dialogue, whether it concerned the people or their behaviours, views, or beliefs. The Socratic method, also known as the dialectical or maieutic method, helped people uncover the truth on their own.

The dialectical method involves acquiring knowledge through debate and seeking the truth by challenging stereotypes and established perceptions. Challenge is the starting point of creation and progress.

The method is processed in two stages. The first phase involves questioning or raising doubts about what is known. Through logic applied to the various prepositions or questions, the validity or contradiction present in thought is sought. Thus, a distinction is made between facts (reality, data) and opinions, which translate into value judgments (personal or social) on a given issue.

In the second step, we seek to advance knowledge, starting from the facts as they are presented and looking for new ideas and new concepts about the issues and problems to solve.

The maieutic method encourages individuals to think for themselves—that is, to ask the questions and produce their own answers. Starting with the knowledge of oneself, one can develop knowledge of the outside world.

Socrates' mother, Phaenarete, was a midwife, and he always compared his dialectical method with the art of midwifery. It is not the midwife who gives birth to the child but the mother. **Similarly, it is not the coach who gives birth to the truth but the coachee**. True knowledge comes from within us. According to Socrates, "giving birth to knowledge" is a natural ability of all human beings. We are all capable of perceiving philosophical truths if we use our minds correctly. Socrates considered it his duty to help his interlocutors arrive at the right conclusion.

"Learning" is, therefore, the process of putting our minds to work and activating the great physical ability to "birth knowledge."

The coaching process

Coaching is the ultimate search for truth through dialogue. The discovery is made by the coachees themselves. It is based on the Socratic assumption that every person holds within them knowledge and truth.

Coaches guide coachees "to give birth to it." They challenge the coachees and motivate them to "learn" and recognise their inexhaustible potential.

Debate over education

Socrates did not consider himself a teacher. He approached his interlocutors and confessed that *he* wanted to learn from *them*. He debated; he did not teach. He asked questions. He listened actively. He never chatted.

From the start, he pretended to be ignorant. He then made his interlocutors discern for themselves the imperfections and weaknesses of their reasoning. Crowded with contradictions, his interlocutors were compelled to recognise their own errors.

Socrates became a philosopher because philosophers strive tirelessly in their quest for more knowledge and truth.

But we should not forget that Socrates was not just a philosopher. He had learned the art of stonemasonry from his father. He was also a soldier, taking part in three campaigns during the Peloponnesian War, where he exhibited bravery and self-sacrifice. He took part in the siege of Potidaea and in the battle of Amphipolis, where he saved the life of Alcibiades.

*"I cannot teach anybody anything;
I can only make them think."*

— SOCRATES[3]

The coaching process

Coaches are tireless truth detectors seeking the truth that people hide within them. They never give up, no matter how difficult the task is. Through this process, they become better themselves. The benefits are mutual.

The process of discovering the truth is refreshing and liberating for everyone.

Coaches have patience, perseverance, and experience from other professions or activities that have played a role in their personal development.

Integrity

Socrates argued that no one can be happy living against their true values and beliefs. For a person to be happy, they need to be aligned with their true potential and desires. This is the meaning of living with integrity.

To live with integrity and find happiness, we need to be aware of our path.

When we can discern what is **good** and **right** for us, we are likely to achieve happiness.

---

[3] This quote is attributes to Socrates. This statement encapsulates Socrates' method of guiding others to discover knowledge through questioning and critical thinking.

The coaching process

Coaches know that the best motivation for people to achieve difficult goals is to understand what really satisfies them and makes them happy.

Coaches facilitate the coachees to discover their authentic self and their motivations.

They then support them to choose the appropriate behaviour that will bring them closer to their dreams. Coaches recognise the great value of integrity, the agreement between our actions and our true thoughts.

People who believe one thing but practice another are unhappy. No one intends to be unhappy.

The conscience of Socrates

Socrates possessed an inner divine voice (*daimonion*—guardian spirit), **the conscience**, that helped him distinguish between right and wrong.

Conscience, for Socrates, represents **right knowledge that leads to right action**.

Socrates used to say that consciousness is a muscle that, when exercised, becomes stronger. He urged all people to acquire consciousness as a guide to choosing the right deeds.

The coaching process

Human consciousness for the coach is our authentic self, our true desires and potential.

When people recognise the importance of living with integrity, in accordance with their true abilities and values, they are more likely to be happy.

In any other case, their inner voice creates guilt, stemming from the torturous feeling of unfulfilled desire or potential.

Internal conflicts arising from unfulfilled personal contracts cause most cases of melancholy and depression in the modern world.

2.3. Aristotle

Aristotle was a student of Plato and a teacher of Alexander the Great. He is considered the most important philosopher and founder of Western philosophy and science.

Aristotle clearly stated why (the reason) and how (the way) we should live. He established the principles of leadership (politics), and he has fanatical researchers and supporters to this day.

Below, I present some excerpts from his teachings and compare them with the relevant theory and practice of coaching.

The search for eudaimonia

As Alexander the Great characteristically said: "I am indebted to my father for living, but to my teacher Aristotle for living well." (*quote attributed to Alexander*)

Aristotle was the first to answer the question of how we should live. According to him, the purpose of life is eudaimonia, the highest good for humans—that is, happiness.

Eudaimonia is a gift from the gods gained through the practice of virtues. A happy life is a life modelled on virtues and the golden mean! Positive psychology is based on the same philosophical idea.

The coaching process

Coaching can help you live a happy, authentic life with a holistic approach, taking care of your body, mind, and soul.

None of the three should monopolise your interest, but all three should be in balance.

> Happiness has no age.
>
> It is never too late to be happy.

The experience

According to Aristotle, the achievement of eudaimonia takes time. True happiness presupposes a full life and, therefore, a long life. As we grow older, we become wiser.

Happiness does not equal short-lived pleasures or moments of bliss. It is something long-lasting. In my opinion, it is closer to prosperity and accomplishment.

The coaching process

For coaching, there is no universal definition of happiness. Each coachee determines enjoyment and happiness in a different way.

Coaching maintains the liberating belief that there is always time to claim the important things in life.

Every experience is useful, regardless of the result, as long as it brings us closer to our higher goal: happiness.

The responsibility of choices

According to Aristotle, people are like plants—they thrive when they find themselves in a suitable soil and climate.

Moreover, they are responsible for their life because they can choose their actions. They have the ability to choose what kind of person they become.

The coaching process

Coaches motivate us to live a happy life—to discover our true self, our abilities, our desires—and to fulfil our higher purpose.

As mentioned above, there is always time for the important things in our lives, no matter when we discover them.

Our life path is full of discoveries and experiences that can lead us to a more authentic and satisfying life. This depends, to a large extent, on our own decisions and actions.

The main pursuit of coaching is human development: the fulfilment of potential and authentic choices, the search for a suitable environment where the individual can shine and bring to the surface their true self.

Human interaction—society

According to Aristotle, people's happiness, success, and life in general is influenced by what happens to other people they care about.

Happiness is achieved by living in a like-minded community. We find our happiness by interacting with the people around us in a well-organised system called "society."

For this reason, we have an obligation to participate and shape this social system. To be **active and responsible citizens**.

The coaching process

In coaching, interacting with others teaches us things about ourselves and is essential in the journey of self-knowledge.

So, we have a duty to set a positive example in society, to live with authenticity and solidarity, to respect our boundaries and other people's boundaries.

Also, we have a responsibility to recognise the benefits of living together in an organised social system, to respect the rules and to overcome obstacles, seeking a smooth and peaceful coexistence.

The right habits create the right character

To increase our chances for eudaimonia, we need to develop from an early age the right character—namely, the right emotions, habits, and moral and intellectual virtues. When we cultivate the above, we create a good, virtuous character.

A "good life" is built on virtues, the qualities of our character that we must practice until they become a way of life.

Aristotelian virtues are intertwined with the most appropriate behaviour in order to achieve eudaimonia, happiness.

The coaching process

According to coaching, our behaviour depends on our character, the human qualities we have acquired from our childhood until today.

Coaches mobilise us to acquire the right character (virtues and values), so that we can support our authentic aspirations and have a happy life.

The principle of the golden mean is accepted by most modern philosophers and psychologists. According to Daniel Goleman, avoiding extremes is achieved through self-regulation, a social skill included in his theory of emotional intelligence.

Another social skill that dominates passions and impulses is self-control. This skill is enhanced by the virtue of wisdom.

To effectively support their coachees, coaches need to remain objective and detached and not get carried away by emotionally charged interactions. Ideally, they should convey understanding and empathy while staying sober.

Authentic human involvement and understanding is the practice of Irvin Yalom, my favourite psychiatrist and psychotherapist.

Eudaimonia and self-actualisation

According to Aristotle, the purpose of life is to pursue eudaimonia through the cultivation of virtues and the utilisation of our abilities.

In his work "Nicomachean Ethics," Aristotle explores the nature of eudaimonia and the various factors that contribute to it. He emphasises the importance of developing good habits and engaging in virtuous actions, rather than simply seeking pleasure or avoiding pain. In order to be happy, it is necessary to pursue personal improvement and do what is right for ourselves and for society as responsible political beings.

The cultivation and utilisation of our abilities leads to eudaimonia, the highest degree of satisfaction in Aristotle's hierarchy.

The coaching process

Similarly, self-actualisation is the highest degree of satisfaction in the hierarchy of needs developed by Abraham Maslow, the psychologist who laid the foundations of modern motivation theory.

Richard Barrett, a highly recognised executive coach and pioneering researcher, developed a similar model to identify the stages of psychological development for each age range.

The highest stage of this ladder after self-actualisation is the pursuit of social participation and contribution.

Coaches support the coachees throughout this path of personal growth and development.

Of course, coaches have not attained perfection. Coaches are, above all, human beings with weaknesses. But what sets them apart is that they systematically receive coaching, mentoring, supervision, or other help whenever needed.

Excellence—*aristeia*

According to Aristotle, excellence, the English translation of the Greek word *aristeia*, is associated with virtuous individuals. They practice virtues and possess the most important intellectual virtue, wisdom, which is knowledge combined with action, practical wisdom or phronesis.

Excellence does not equal "perfection," as it has wrongly prevailed in modern society. It has more to do with action and efficiency, with improving and utilising the abilities of each person, not obsessing over perfection.

Excellence is the way of life that leads to eudaimonia.

Someone who is excellent exhibits all three of the following behaviours:

- researcher and philosopher searching for knowledge and truth
- joyous and fun person who enjoys everyday life in society
- free and responsible citizen who participates in actions that affect the human community.

In other words, perfection does not come from knowledge but from its practice.

> *"Because the purpose [of political science] is not knowledge, but practice."*
>
> — ARISTOTLE, POLITICS, BOOK III (PART 1)

The coaching process

For coaches, excellence is the purpose of life. We believe that every human being has the right to pursue perfection—that is, to make full use of their abilities and to fulfil their authentic desires.

Coaches support the coachees throughout this painful but liberating journey.

Prudence—practical wisdom—phronesis

According to Aristotle, a wise person is someone who pursues knowledge and at the same time applies it in practice. Prudence is one of Aristotle's most important intellectual virtues, the sum of wisdom (knowledge) and practice.

Practical wisdom is sound judgement that helps people distinguish between good and bad deeds, between good and bad habits.

The coaching process

Coaches seek the truth to engage you in action. They want you to change your life, to live with integrity according to your authentic needs and abilities. And to achieve this, it is necessary to start practicing it.

An old habit is replaced only by a new one.

Coaches remain by your side throughout your effort to acquire a new way of life, motivating you and energising you.

2.4. The convergence of Ancient Greek philosophies

Ancient Greek philosophy, in terms of **why** (the **reason**) we live and **how** (the **way**) we should live, can be summarised as follows:

Why: We live to pursue **well-being—eudaimonia**.

How: We live with **excellence**. An excellent person is someone who lives with **practical wisdom (prudence)**, pursuing truth and **knowledge** and transforming it into **action**, someone who practices **virtue** and goodwill (positive attitude).

In conclusion, excellence means living with **ethos**, practicing a virtuous behaviour until the new behaviour becomes a habit.

"It is quality, not quantity, of life that matters."

— ARISTOTLE[4]

Excellence, for ancient philosophers as well as modern coaches, is a quality that is unique for every human being.

In my opinion, it also depends on how consistent our practice of virtues is.

The goal of coaching is harmony and balance. Harmony has to do with integrity and balance with self-realisation.

People's uniqueness is the greatness of human superiority and the culmination of every ancient or modern philosophical reflection.

"Moderation in all things."

— CLEOBULUS OF LINDOS[5]
ONE OF THE SEVEN SAGES OF
ANCIENT GREECE (6TH C. BC)

---

4   It is often attributed to the ancient Greek philosopher Aristotle. However, this specific quote does not appear in any of his surviving works.

5   It is attributed to the ancient Greek philosopher Cleobulus of Lindos. This quote is often associated with his teachings on the virtue of moderation. However, since Cleobulus lived in the 6th century BCE, the exact source or citation for this quote may be difficult to determine.

2.5. Emotions

According to classic philosophers, **passion**, **love**, and **fear** are instincts with which nature has endowed us to protect us and strengthen the perpetuation of mankind.

These emotions are useful for the above purposes, but their excess may bring the opposite results, such as paralysis, confusion, and finally, resignation.

According to **Daniel Goleman's emotional intelligence** theory, emotions guide our behaviour, our thoughts, our decisions, and, of course, our performance. First, we feel, and then we think.

Therefore, it is impossible to ignore the emotions that we or the environment create in people, as well as our own emotions.

According to Daniel Goleman, emotional intelligence has the following dimensions:

- self-awareness
- self-regulation
- motivation
- empathy
- social skills.

In short, it has to do with the following skills: awareness, justification, management, and expression of emotions for the benefit of ourselves and others.

Coaching can help improve and enhance these skills.

Emotional intelligence refers to the ability to recognise and understand our own emotions and those of others, then manage them effectively and, finally, constantly generate motivation for ourselves and others.

Emotional intelligence skills build the foundation for mutual trust, which is essential for any communication.

Goleman, through continuous scientific research, has shown that 80% of an individual's effectiveness is due to the ability of emotional intelligence. In other words, the IQ level contributes no more than 20% to an individual's ability to function effectively and successfully (from Goleman's book *Emotional Intelligence: Why It Can Matter More Than IQ*).

According to **Irvin Yalom**, the great existential psychotherapist, empathy is the most powerful tool we have in our effort to connect with other human beings.

In his book, *Staring at the Sun: Overcoming the Dread of Death*, he states that "empathy is what binds the bond between people and allows us to feel to a great extent what someone else is feeling. Relationships are usually built on mutual self-disclosure" (2008, p. 191).

Brené Brown, a great scholar known for her research on emotions, in her book, *Atlas of the Heart*, says beautifully that empathy is the tool of compassion, which is one of the most crucial feelings for achieving meaningful connections.

For Ancient Greek philosophers, self-control and moderation do not equal a life without emotions, as some might assume. On the contrary, emotions are an inalienable part of the Ancient Greek proposition of life, but without their excess or deficiency—only as much as it is necessary so that they do not deprive us of our freedom of choice, our self-esteem, and our claim to a meaningful life.

The coaching process

Here is an interesting difference. In coaching, the coachees can choose and decide how to manage the emotions that result from specific desires and choices, as long as they are ready for the consequences.

Self-accountability is cultivated through coaching discussions. The coachees are responsible for their decisions and actions and, clearly, for the consequences.

Coaches are dedicated emotion detectors. They observe with great attention every emotional reaction of their interlocutor. This is because the emotions provide useful information for the evaluation and progress of each coaching discussion.

2.6. Summary: philosophy vs coaching

1. Ancient Greek philosophers, motivated by the love of knowledge, sought answers to existential issues, such as why and how we should live to honour the purpose of our existence.
2. Socrates was the first philosopher to explore human nature and the soul. The science of coaching is human-centred and explores our motivations and related behaviour.

3. Socrates put the search for our intrinsic truth at the centre of his philosophy, just like coaching.
4. Socrates considered the pursuit of self-knowledge a starting point but also a long journey requiring knowledge and experience.
5. Socrates conceded the infinity of human ignorance, and coaching acknowledges that human behaviour is often indicated by habits or false assumptions, social conventions, or restrictive beliefs.
6. Socrates arrived at the truth through debate. The Socratic method leads people to discover the truth on their own. The coach is a tireless truth detector. Practicing truth-seeking is refreshing and liberating.
7. Socratic inquiry aims to reveal the limitations and assumptions upon which people lead their lives. Coaching helps us recognise and reposition our limitations on a new, more substantial and authentic basis.
8. Socrates did not teach; he debated. He constantly asked questions, but he did not give answers. He listened carefully, without talking, and guided his interlocutors to discern the imperfections and weaknesses of their reasoning. The coach does the same.
9. Socrates believed that philosophers should see beyond the apparent. Coaching helps people see beyond social prejudices or false assumptions.
10. According to Socrates, no one does evil knowing that it is evil. There are no good or bad behaviours. Every human being is accountable for the behaviour that benefits or destroys them.
11. Socrates, with his martyrdom, taught us that we should take responsibility for our ideas and actions. Coaches clarify at the beginning of every coaching relationship that the coachees are responsible for their actions and consequences.

12. Socrates believed that people should live with integrity—that is, according to their true potential and desires. Coaches believe people get motivated to overcome obstacles when they discover what makes them happy.
13. Socrates believed in an inner divine voice, the conscience, that dictated what was right and just to him. For coaching, the human conscience is the authentic self. People who are taught to live with integrity will continue to do so and be happy; otherwise, they will be tormented by internal conflicts such as guilt.
14. Aristotle clearly stated why and how a person should live. According to Aristotle, we must seek happiness—and a happy life is a life of virtue! Coaching helps you live a happy life in a nurturing environment, with your virtues (qualities) and values (desires) as reference points.
15. According to Aristotle, true happiness is enduring and is achieved through cultivating and utilising our abilities. Discovering, developing, and using our skills is the ultimate goal of coaching.
16. Aristotelian eudaimonia is achieved through interaction. We find happiness when we relate to those around us. According to coaching, human interaction is essential for the journey of self-discovery.
17. According to Aristotle, the purpose of life is to achieve happiness through the practice of virtues, to become a better person and promote positive behaviour patterns. The virtuous person pursues the golden mean and avoids the extremes of excess and deficiency. Coaches support the coachees to develop the right character to achieve their goals.
18. According to Aristotle, the wise seek knowledge and apply it in practice. Coaching helps you acquire the proper habits that will help you change, transform, and achieve your goals.

POINTS TO REMEMBER FROM STEP 2

- The methodology of coaching has a lot in common with Classic Greek philosophy, as expressed by Socrates, Plato, and Aristotle.
- The essence and the deepest meaning of life is the pursuit of eudaimonia.
- Coaching leadership brings out the best in people. The Coach Leader sets the example for a sustainable, ethical, and human-centred society characterised by practical wisdom, one of the greatest Aristotelian virtues.
- The art and science of coaching goes back a long way and is constantly updated by incorporating the most modern and effective theories from other sciences, such as philosophy and positive psychology.

YOUR TURN

Immediate action I will take:

Are there any obstacles? If so, what are they?

How will I overcome each obstacle?

STEP 3

THE PATH TO A NEW LEADER PROFILE

"A new existential reflection is born based on inner emancipation and the pursuit of a higher purpose for the common good."

— BARBARA ASIMAKOPOULOU

PURPOSE

In the **third step**, I present the conditions that pave the way for the new leader profile: the everyday leader who strives for inner emancipation, who is always a coach, who possesses distinct human qualities (virtues) and skills. The Coach Leader who envisions an ethical, sustainable society and happy people.

3.1. The new conditions

We are experiencing global changes and significant risks. All social, political, cultural, technological, and economic environments are in a state of transition. In times like these, characterised by volatility and instability, we must be resilient and prepared for the unexpected. Are we, though? Everyday experience suggests we are not.

There is often a perception that everything will change without us having to change individually. In theory, this is called "resistance to change"; in practice, it is known as indifference, irresponsibility, or lack of vision.

> Adapting to change is not defeat.
>
> It is an opportunity to move forward.

According to **Peter Senge**, Senior Lecturer in Leadership and Sustainability at MIT Sloan School of Management, "People are open to change, as long as ... they don't have to change themselves."

According to him, **change is a natural consequence of evolution; it happens because it simply needs to happen**. The sooner we realise it, the better we will deal with change, its demands, and its consequences.

In addition, we need to accept that **real change first begins with ourselves**. We need to focus inwards, discover ourselves and resurface as better leaders, better partners, better entrepreneurs, better parents.

Reassessment, reconstruction, reinvention, and action. It is an individual and team sport where the **coach** plays an important role!

> The coach inspires you to discover your best self; they empower you and help you achieve your dreams.

3.2. The characteristics of the new leader

Life is full of challenges. Every challenge conceals a threat but also an opportunity. Coach Leaders are tasked with discovering opportunities and co-creating with their team an attractive destination that will inspire them to fight and claim it. It is a race of endurance, a **battle of peace**, not revenge, a battle that will bring the Coach Leader and their team closer to true values and their true selves.

Businesses and organisations need allies to successfully meet challenges. They need **teams that deliver, consent, and commit to mutual benefits**.

They need responsible, engaged, and accountable executives with enhanced communication skills, such as the ability to hold effective discussions, persuasion and influence, active listening, and eloquence in public speaking. Finally, there is the need to acquire new skills, such as adaptability, resilience, powerful questioning, and the art of storytelling.

Resilience

Leaders, like all people, need to adapt to the unique requirements of each environment to practice resilience.

In other words, they must alternate between strategies and recalibrate to their core values without breaking.

The virtues

The new leader has distinct qualities: Aristotle's intellectual and moral virtues, such as bravery, magnificence, magnanimity, practical wisdom, and justice.

It becomes clear that the new leader needs a new worldview. In this book, I present a type of leadership, **centred around humans who aspire to live a "good life,"** as Socrates first suggested in his teachings, and as the science of modern coaching advocates.

The art and science of **coaching** helps current and future leaders develop first themselves and then their team and their successors.

> The coveted inner emancipation of the Coach Leader is achieved through coaching.

3.3. What sets the modern leader apart

According to **Jim Collins**, ideal leaders who lead their businesses from good to great (in his book of the same title) with lasting results are: "a paradoxical mix of personal modesty and strong professional will. They resemble more to Lincoln or Socrates than to Paton or Caesar."

The existing theory and practice of leadership is indeed rich. What I am quoting below is based on selected, world-renowned leadership theories, enriched, of course, by my own interpretation and elaboration.

Examples: Aristotle, Sun Tzu, Friedrich Wilhelm Nietzsche, Ken Blanchard, Stephen Covey, Jim Collins, Jerry I. Porras, Daniel Goleman, Richard Boyatzis, Dimitris Bourantas, Haridimos Tsoukas, Sir John Whitmore, Marshall Goldsmith, Richard Barrett, Sally Helgesen, and Brené Brown.

In addition to the theory, research, and practice of the above philosophers, consultants, professors, and scientists, I have also been influenced by known or less-known positive leadership figures who stand out on a larger or smaller scale.

They all embody leadership qualities that are extremely valuable for current or future leaders.

Examples: Theodoros Kolokotronis, Ioannis Kapodistrias, Charilaos Trikoupis, Eleftherios Venizelos, Konstantinos Karamanlis, Nelson Mandela, Margaret Thatcher, Gandhi, Angela Merkel, Barack

Obama, Katerina Sakellaropoulou, Theodore Papalexopoulos, and Prodromos Papavassiliou, my life and business partner. I also mention Tony Meloto, the founder of Gawad Kalinga, a volunteer movement to fight poverty in the Philippines, who is an amazing example of social entrepreneurship.

3.3.1. From personal ambition to vision

Modern leaders need to create compelling visions that go beyond their personal ambitions and foster the common good. To this end, they invite people's participation in designing and shaping the vision and the long-term or short-term goals needed to achieve it. This way, they create a **community to which everyone would like to belong**.

3.3.2. Role model for future leaders

Plutarch (46-120 AD), Greek philosopher, biographer and historian, mentioned the value of being inspired from the example of ethical people (his book "Parallel Lives" is series of parallel biographies of great men).

In a time of crisis, all eyes are on the leader. This means that the leader has power and influence but, at the same time, a huge responsibility. Depending on their vision, they can lead their followers to destruction or victory. Their example also inspires future leaders.

Excellence according to Aristotle

According to Aristotle, the leader seeks excellence on a daily basis. Perfection (excellence) is not something universal or strictly demarcated; it is **reaching the full potential of yourself and the people of your team**.

Contemporary American psychologist **Martin Seligman** confirms Aristotle's findings with his research.

Aristotle's excellence is **how** to achieve eudaimonia, and eudaimonia is the orientation of life—the "**what**," which includes the "**why**," the meaning of every person's life.

Excellence is achieved through the practice of moral and intellectual virtues, through "hexis" habituation with daily and continuous practice. Only then will the new behaviour become a new habit. In his work "Nicomachean Ethics" Aristotle explores the nature of virtue, moral character, and the development of excellence through habitual action.

> Excellence for Aristotle, as consciousness for Socrates, is a muscle that needs to be exercised daily to remain strong.

"Habit is a second nature."

— CICERO[6], ROMAN PHILOSOPHER (106–43 BC)

3.3.3. Aristotelian virtues and ethos

The word "**ethos**" derives from the word "hexis," which means addiction (habit).

---

[6] It's often associated with Cicero's teachings on habituation and the development of character. As such, the quote is a general reflection of Cicero's philosophy and does not come from a specific chapter or passage within his writings.

According to Socrates—the "scientist of Ethics," as Aristotle calls him—**ethos** is the good character acquired through the practice of moral virtues and, ultimately, their addiction.

Aristotle, who was the best student of Plato's Academy, developed the teaching of moral and intellectual virtues to such an extent that his theory retains its freshness to this day and, most importantly, gives us the **best reference frame** to achieve personal and social happiness.

I analyse these virtues more below because I strongly believe that if people and especially leaders adopt them, the human race will gain sustainability and perspective.

Aristotle presents the moral and intellectual virtues in his work *Nicomachean Ethics*, which is said to have been written for his son, Nicomachus.

The "Nicomachean Ethics" is a significant philosophical treatise in which Aristotle delves into the nature of ethics, human flourishing, and the development of virtues.

The work consists of ten books, with each book containing multiple chapters. Aristotle explores various aspects of ethics and virtues throughout the entire work.

To gain insights into Aristotle's discussion on virtues, it is helpful to focus on Books II to IV of the "Nicomachean Ethics."

Book II addresses the concept of moral virtue and Aristotle's exploration of the "Doctrine of the Mean." He discusses how virtues lie between extremes and emphasises the importance of finding the right balance in human action and character.

Book III delves further into the examination of specific moral virtues, such as courage, temperance, and generosity. Aristotle explores their nature, characteristics, and how they relate to living a virtuous life.

Book IV extends the discussion on moral virtues and introduces the idea of justice as a virtue. Aristotle explores the various forms of justice and their role in a well-ordered society.

It is important to mention two important parameters that will help us understand his work:

1. It is addressed to the average Greek citizen of his time.
2. It is adapted to the realities of the Greek city-state.

The practice of moral and intellectual virtues, according to Aristotle, aims at shaping a good character and achieving personal and social **eudaimonia**.

Virtue and the golden mean

According to Aristotle, virtue is an intermediate state between two extremes: excess and deficiency. This "golden mean" is determined by one's judgment and reason. Virtue is the pursuit of balance and moderation. Only balance and moderation ensure happiness and harmony in everyday life.

But it should be noted that the intermediate state does not equal mediocrity (mediocre person = lacks interest, boring, few abilities) but instead is a claim to excellence. Excellence is the result of practicing virtues: socially acceptable qualities that are intermediate states between excess and deficiency.

The "wise" claim moderation and virtue by practicing the **right thing**, which is determined by reason—what is needed, at the right time, in the right way, with the right people, for the right reason and, most importantly, always for the greater good, not just personal benefit.

As Aristotle characteristically says, we can expect to experience feelings of anger, fear, desire, pity, happiness, or sadness "**in relation**" to things or people. But it is important to have a clear goal—which, in this case, is to pursue moderation and virtue.

We should not be discouraged if, in some cases, we have a tendency towards excess or deficiency. When we have a stable point of reference—virtues and reason—we know how we should behave, and we are more likely to approach the ideal. Even if we move away, we can always return to it.

According to Aristotle, failure (distance from the golden mean) is meant to teach us. The important thing is to know the goal and pursue it no matter how many times we fail.

Analysing the virtues today, we come to realise how timeless they are. I consider them necessary for the Coach Leader because I genuinely believe that their practice ensures a happy life and, at the same time, transforms us into **ethical and inspired leaders** of a sustainable society.

In summary, according to Aristotle, **ethics is a set of good habits**, attitudes, and behaviours acquired through practice. They constitute moral and intellectual virtues.

Intellectual virtues

Intellectual virtues are the fundamental qualities of the reason that help us discover the truth and adopt the appropriate behaviour. Intellectual virtues can be taught and depend on the effectiveness of the teacher.

Intellectual virtues include "**techne**" (artistic or technical knowledge), "**episteme**" (scientific knowledge), "**sophia**" (philosophical knowledge, philosophy), "**wisdom**" (practical reason), and "**noesis**" (judgement, intuitive reasoning).

The greatest of intellectual virtues is **practical wisdom** (phronesis): theoretical knowledge combined with practical knowledge. This is the reason that precedes the practice of virtues, the right judgment of good and bad things, the correct use of word and deed to gain experience of good things.

Practical wisdom is necessary for all other virtues because moral virtues, to be put into practice, require wisdom. It ensures that the purpose, in addition to being moral, is also reasonable. It also determines the manner and means by which the goal will be performed.

Moral virtues

Moral virtues presuppose the cultivation of the soul and depend solely on the person and their will to practice them.

According to Aristotle, we do not naturally possess virtues; we acquire them through practice and addiction. Moral virtues are the product of habit.

> *"The moral virtues are produced in us neither by nature nor against nature. Nature, indeed, prepares in us the ground for their reception, but their complete formation is the product of habit."*
>
> — ARISTOTLE, *NICOMACHEAN ETHICS*, BOOK II, CHAPTER 1 (1103A23-25)

Excellence is achieved through will and perseverance in the practice of virtue.

Some of the moral virtues are courage, temperance, generosity, and meekness.

Intellectual virtues help us find the truth. Moral virtues help us behave in specific situations.

In my opinion, intellectual virtues represent the rational part of the soul (logos), and moral virtues help us understand emotions (thymos) and manage the desiring part of the soul (eros).

> Aristotelian virtues are the best "UNIVERSAL FRAMEWORK" of behaviour, an ideal point of reference for human expression and attitude. The constant pursuit of these virtues leads to personal and social eudaimonia.

Example: The virtue of bravery shows us the ideal way to manage fear: to be courageous when it is necessary and as much as it is reasonable.

Too much bravery makes us insolent; not enough makes us cowards. Experiencing fear when we perceive danger does not make us cowards—facing danger or any other misfortune when and as much as it is necessary makes us brave. The virtue of bravery is strengthened when we serve a greater purpose.

Here is a list of Aristotelian virtues to help you clearly understand appropriate behaviour (the golden mean) and inappropriate behaviour (excess and deficiency).

VIRTUE (the golden mean)	EXCESS	DEFICIENCY
Bravery: Proper management of fear and courage, not fearing death, showing courage in hardships and fearlessness in danger. A brave person is also characterised by patience, composure, hard work, perseverance, self-confidence.	Insolence, excessive risk.	Cowardice.

VIRTUE (the golden mean)	EXCESS	DEFICIENCY
Liberality: Properly managing resources, money, knowledge, information, material goods, energy, generosity. Investing in good things even if they are not profitable, solving financial differences. Generosity is accompanied by mildness of character, hospitality, charity, friendship, and tastefulness (appreciating what is good and virtuous).	Prodigality: Having no hope of salvation; promiscuous, wasteful.	Illiberality: Inner slavery (e.g., avarice).
Truthfulness: Being truthful; love of truth; being honest with yourself and enjoying inner balance.	Arrogance: Excessive selfishness, self-deception; misleading.	Ignorance: The pretence of ignorance, irony, lack of understanding of truth = lie.
Magnanimity: Being capable of enduring happiness and misery, honour, and dishonour. Behaving in a good way, with depth and breadth of soul. A simple, kind, and true person.	Vanity, conceit: Considering yourself worthy of greatness while not being worthy of it.	Pusillanimity: Considering yourself unworthy of greatness while being worthy of it.

VIRTUE (the golden mean)	EXCESS	DEFICIENCY
Magnificence: Being suited to becoming great. Refers to social contribution and large projects of public benefit.	Vulgarity: Inelegance, brutality, illusion of grandeur. Ostentatiousness, contributing an exceptionally large amount that is not needed.	Pettiness: Worthy of being small, insignificant; miserableness, bad taste.
Wittiness: Ability to turn things in your favour, intelligence, humour, resourcefulness, ingenuity, eloquence. Ability to make jokes and enjoy the jokes of others.	Buffoonery: Blasphemy, indecency. Being repugnant, clownish. Acting obsequiously to achieve what you want.	Boorishness: Unrefined, lacking cultivation, crude, rugged, blunt, rigid.
Temperance: Self-control, prudence, moderation, having a healthy mind. Proper management of desires and emotions. Not getting carried away by the pleasures of the senses. Loving order. Being characterised by good manners, decency, respect, and piety.	Licentiousness: Indiscipline, incivility, lack of control.	Insensibility: Having no desire, apathy, inability to grasp your environment.

VIRTUE (the golden mean)	EXCESS	DEFICIENCY
Meekness: Mildness, calmness, ability to not get carried away by anger, ability to manage anger in terms of intensity, frequency, and mood.	Irascibility: Quarrelsome, morose.	Lack of spirit: Lack of anger or reaction.
Friendliness: Amiability, managing sociability, disposition for friendliness, kindness and mutual reciprocity, gratitude, a soul in two bodies.	Obsequiousness or flattery: Hanging around for food or material goods and displaying slavish behaviour, the source of which is insecurity.	Cantankerousness: Aversion, the enemy, the one outside the walls, unlikability; the source is a constantly defensive attitude = anxiety.
Nemesis: Ability to distribute responsibilities, to manage effectively and fairly. The root of this word is the law = *nomos* in Greek.	Envy: Desire to have a skill, financial status, possession, or other thing belonging to someone else.	Epicaricacy: Malicious enjoyment, feeling joy for the sorrow or misfortune of another (schadenfreude).
Special Justice: Ability to claim goods according to their value, to distribute the benefits or losses between themselves and others with justice.	More benefit (profit) than necessary, more damage than necessary, greed (deception, cunningness).	Less benefit (gain) than necessary, less damage than necessary (loss).

VIRTUE (the golden mean)	EXCESS	DEFICIENCY
Sincerity: Truth in words and deeds, admitting to having what you really have and being who you really are.	Boastfulness: Pride, vanity, pretending to be more than you are, misappropriating possessions.	Understatement: Concealing, demeaning, or degrading yourself with regard to who you are or what you have.
Honor: Healthy ambition; managing your desire for honour, recognition in a positive way.	Excessive ambition: Unhealthy ambition; excessive desire for honour, recognition.	Unambitiousness: Excessive lack of desire for honour; depreciation indifference.

According to Aristoteles, the intellectual virtues—judgment, practical wisdom, and general justice—don't have a golden mean or the two extremes of excess and deficiency. Practical wisdom applies to all moral virtues. It helps you choose the right steps to reach the goal.

Justice is the mother of the virtues; it connects and is conferred within all the virtues. So this kind of justice is, of course, a perfect virtue, but not in a general and absolute way—only with the addition of "in relation to the other."

This is also why justice is often considered the greatest virtue. "Neither the evening star nor the morning star is so bright and wonderful." Also, speaking proverbially, we say, "justice shuts up all the virtues."

Justice is a perfect—to the greatest extent—virtue because it is an exercise/application of perfect virtue. It is perfect because the people with this virtue can also use it in their relationships with other people, not only for themselves.

We cannot serve justice if we do not adequately manage the moral and intellectual virtues. All the virtues aim at justice so that there may be balance.

Therefore, special justice is not related to the law, as happens in general justice, but with equality. Thus, justice appears as a moral justification of inequalities. According to Aristotle, there are three types of individual justice—distributive, corrective, and compensatory justice—which are governed by the principle of equality.

Special justice has deviations of the golden mean, extremes depending on claiming the goods or managing the distribution of losses and benefits. Observing the laws, customs, and traditions; telling the truth and keeping promises.

The virtuous person's (i.e., the one who practices the virtues) feeling is balanced.

The virtues are all interconnected. Virtues must become second nature to us; that is, we must forget who we were before them. *Learn and unlearn.*

According to Aristotle, the act as an opportunity to acquire virtues is not enough; the outcome of the action also plays an important role. The outcome should create delight, euphoria, and eudaimonia.

Leaders must practice moral virtues as well as intellectual virtues.

Eudaimonia

According to Aristotle, the virtuous individual who practices moral and intellectual virtues acquires the greatest good, eudaimonia: a state of excellence characterised by flourishing across a lifetime.

In terms of its etymology, eudaimonia is an abstract noun derived from the words *eû* (good, well) and *daímōn* (dispenser, tutelary deity), the latter referring maybe to a minor deity or a guardian spirit.

The virtuous person practices excellence. Thus, excellence leads to eudaimonia.

According to Aristotle, eudaimonia is reached through a life of pleasure, science, political activity, and philosophy.

According to **Mihaly Csikszentmihalyi**, an American psychologist and author of *Flow*, the modern definition of happiness is the ineffable feeling enjoyed by creative people (artists, writers, musicians, etc.) when they are so immersed in their activity that all other concerns or worries are set aside.

I believe Aristotle's eudaimonia is close to Mihaly Csikszentmihalyi's flow state.

3.4. Characteristics of an effective coach

Below, I present the characteristics of the ideal coach.

Self-knowledge

The ideal coach identifies their strengths and weaknesses and pursues self-improvement for their personal benefit, the benefit of their clients, and the benefit of society at large.

Self-development through coaching

Self-knowledge is a gift acquired through a variety of opportunities, such as learning, experience, and social interaction. Interacting with and seeking support from another coach will allow you to enjoy the benefits of coaching: personal and professional progress, emancipation, development, and overcoming internal and external obstacles. Coaches that do not use or trust coaching for personal development are either perfect (which is impossible) or highly arrogant and do not offer the best to their clients, since they do not offer it to themselves.

A sincere holistic interest in people and the achievement of their goals

The ideal coach aims for a relationship of creative cooperation based on trust and freedom of thought. They stand by their clients, demonstrating a genuine interest and care.

Active listening
Active listening is one of the most important coaching skills.

The ideal coach is alert to what the coachees say or do not say, allowing them to make revelations about themselves and their concerns. In the next step, we will learn more about this skill, which is essential for all people.

The art of questioning

Coaches ask insightful questions to uncover the truth.

They practice the dialectical method of Socrates and are 100% present in every relationship.

Fully present

They are fully focused on the coaching relationship—mentally, emotionally, and physically—to benefit the coachees as much as possible. Coaches should be vulnerable and empathetic and, thus, emotionally connected and compassionate. Moreover, they must practice the virtue of temperance and show sincere understanding and caring.

Effective communication

Coaches use effective communication tools and techniques, such as reflection on past actions (feedback) and constructive guidance on future actions (feedforward). In the next step, we will talk more about this skill.

Trustworthiness

Trust is the necessary background for effective communication and meaningful connection, as Brené Brown says. Coachees should feel free to confess whatever they want about the coaching relationship or their coach. This is not the case, however, on the part of the coach.

Moral principles

Coaches possess a character that reflects the moral and intellectual virtues of classical philosophers, such as practical wisdom, bravery, justice, and temperance.

Respect towards the coachee

Coaches respect the coachee's diversity and choices. Coachees make decisions based on their personal experiences and aspirations, and the coach is always there to show respect and support, working more like a mirror than a critic, an empathetic and compassionate adult challenger and facilitator. Each failure or success brings the coachee closer to their goals. The coachee will win either way because they will learn from both successes and failures.

Inner balance

Coaches have self-knowledge and self-confidence and follow the path to inner balance. They realise the important things in life and have no repressed desires. Coaches are aware of their strengths or weaknesses and work on them to achieve the coveted emotional, mental, and physical balance and serve each client to the maximum.

Culture and aesthetics

Coaches are kind lovers of learning with good manners. They want to set an example for an ethical and civilised society. I believe that culture is a divine principle of life, and I dare say that it is interwoven with the aesthetics of every people. The constant deterioration of aesthetics truly saddens me—aesthetics of speech, behaviour, appearance, movement, creation, space, choices, and more. People's civilisation can be measured by the above. It is no coincidence that art, science, philosophy, theatre, music, poetry, and architecture flourished in the Classical period and the Golden Age of Greece.

Constant growth

Coaches pursue ongoing development to support people to the maximum. They gain new knowledge and experience through training, travelling, and interaction with other professionals and different cultures.

They motivate coachees toward liberation and inner emancipation

Coachees are encouraged to act and take ownership of their actions. Inner emancipation begins with taking full responsibility for the consequences of our actions and choices. For this to happen, coachees need to be aware of their needs, values, and motives. They must cultivate virtues such as practical wisdom, justice, bravery, and temperance (self-control), the fundamental virtues of Stoics.

According to the dictionary of distinguished professor of linguistics, G. Babiniotis, emancipation is synonymous with liberation, independence, autonomy, and, in a metaphorical sense, liberation from the constraints of ignorance and un-enlightenment.

I strongly believe that inner emancipation liberates our good self from internal obstacles—fear, limiting beliefs, prejudices, low self-esteem, and lack of perspective—that hinder our creative expression and growth. Its opposite is being manipulated by and enslaved to ourselves, our relationships, and our environment.

Inner emancipation is the liberation of our good self from internal obstacles hindering creative expression and growth.

Leader characteristics	Coach characteristics
• pursues a higher purpose beyond personal ambition • inspires vision • is a role model for future leaders • cares for developing new leaders • pursues excellence and eudaimonia for themselves and their team • manifests the moral and intellectual virtues of Aristotle • advocates for justice • demonstrates bravery • displays practical wisdom • maintains self-control • participates in activities • motivates and encourages • acknowledges the team and each individual separately • co-creates a vision that inspires • co-creates goals and action plans • co-decides • asks for and strengthens accountability • shows empathy and compassion	• aims at human development • brings out the best in people • demonstrates self-knowledge • pursues personal development coaching • displays a genuine interest in people, their holistic improvement, and the achievement of their goals • pursues a creative relationship of cooperation based on trust and freedom of thought • practices active listening • asks powerful questions • is 100% present in every relationship • communicates effectively • is trustworthy • practices Aristotle's moral and intellectual virtues • respects the coachees and their choices • displays self-control, empathy, and compassion—when fully present • provides feedback • models self-confidence, personal balance, and inner emancipation

Leader characteristics	Coach characteristics
• gives feedback and feedforward • demonstrates active listening • is resilient and embraces change.	• is a lover of culture, learning, and aesthetics • has good manners and is courteous • undertakes ongoing training and development • respects the diversity of each coachee • otivates the coachee to act and take ownership of their actions • strengthens accountability.

POINTS TO REMEMBER FROM STEP 3

- The current fragile and volatile situation of globalised economy and society imposes a collective reflection on the conditions of human survival.
- The disastrous consequences of excess and uncontrolled "progress" give birth to a new existential reflection based on inner emancipation and the pursuit of a higher purpose for the common good.
- People who hold positions of influence bear the greatest responsibility for this redemptive change: to first transform themselves and then others, to adopt virtues and competencies (like resilience) that will allow them to bring about change.
- Socrates is the greatest teacher of all time.
- Aristotle is the greatest teacher on leadership, even to this day.
- If you want change, you first implement it yourself and then motivate and assist your team to change as well.

YOUR TURN

Immediate action I will take:

Are there any obstacles? If so, what are they?

How will I overcome each obstacle?

"Leaders who ignore coaching are passing up a powerful tool: its impact on climate and performance are markedly positive."

— DR. DANIEL GOLEMAN
AMERICAN PSYCHOLOGIST, CONSULTANT, AUTHOR
AND FORMER PROFESSOR AT HARVARD UNIVERSITY

STEP 4

THE COACH LEADER

"The Coach Leader envisions an ethical, sustainable society and happy people."

— BARBARA ASIMAKOPOULOU

PURPOSE

It is universally accepted that the viability of businesses, organisations, and societies depends largely on their leaders and, more specifically, what makes up their profile and behaviour (knowledge, experiences, values, characteristics, and skills).

The purpose of the fourth step is to present the **structural competencies** that distinguish a Coach Leader from any other leader. The Coach Leader embodies the characteristics needed by today's world to ensure its sustainability and the eight ICF competencies of the modern professional coach.

These structural competencies are the DNA of the Coach Leader; they ensure the quality and uniqueness of the Coach Leader's life and practice.

Skills such as **active listening** (ICF Core Competence #6), **powerful questioning**, and **effective communication** (ICF Core Competence #7) play a prominent role.

I also include two important competencies that, in my opinion, mark the behaviour of the Coach Leader: **recognising and rewarding people's efforts** and **creative conflict resolution** through a coaching approach.

In the first part of this step, I present the desired characteristics of the modern leader. In the second part, I list the characteristics of the professional coach. In the third part, I describe the characteristics that constitute the ideal **Coach Leader**.

In the fourth and final part of this step, I delve more into the structural skills that will help you practice and become an ideal Coach Leader.

4.1. The Coach Leader profile

We will now examine the origins of this leadership profile and how the characteristics of the professional coach combined with the features of the modern leader result in the Coach Leader's profile.

4.1.1. Definitions—sources

Paul Hersey and **Kenneth Blanchard** were the first to describe coaching leadership as a leadership style in the late 1960s. In 2002, **Daniel Goleman** included coaching leadership in his six proposed leadership styles. In 2006, **Richard Boyatzis**, **Melvin Smith**, and **Nancy Blaize** presented coaching leadership as a powerful catalyst for leadership effectiveness. In 2013, Daniel Goleman resumed the conversation with a resounding article, "Don't Write Off the Coaching Leadership Style," and his book *Focus: The Hidden Driver of Excellence*.

The **clearest definition of the Coach Leader**, in my opinion, is that of Daniel Goleman.

According to him, a Coach Leader:

- helps employees recognise their unique capabilities, as well as their weaknesses, and combine them with their personal and professional expectations

- encourages employees to set long-term personal development goals and make an action plan to achieve them
- agrees upon and assigns employees roles and responsibilities while providing ample feedback.

Leaders who ignore coaching leadership lose a powerful tool that has a positive effect on their work environment and performance.

> *"The leader of the past was a person who knew how to tell. The leader of the future will be a person who knows how to ask."*
>
> — PETER F. DRUCKER (1909-2005)
> AUSTRIAN-AMERICAN FAMOUS MANAGEMENT CONSULTANT AND AUTHOR

4.1.2. The obstacles

Many leaders claim that they lack time for the slow and painstaking task of coaching people and helping them grow. I would say that the above hesitation is due to the fact that they have not experienced a coaching session themselves.

A coaching session with a trained and experienced professional coach would immediately change their mind. They would surely recognise the effectiveness and dynamics of coaching.

Experience shows that even one session is enough to achieve a change of mind. This is confirmed by all my clients who initially had their reservations.

4.1.3. Why coaching leadership?

Many companies have realised the positive impact of coaching leadership and are trying to incorporate it into the structural skills of their executives. In some organisations, a significant portion of their annual bonuses is linked to the growth of their executives.

Richard Boyatzis, Melvin Smith, and Nancy Blaize, in their article, "Developing sustainable leaders through coaching and compassion," published on 2006, state the following:

"By integrating recent findings in affective neuroscience and biology with well documented research on leadership and stress, we offer a more holistic approach to leadership development. We argue here that leader sustainability is adversely affected by the psychological and physiological effects of chronic power stress associated with the performance of the leadership role. We further contend, however, that when leaders experience compassion through coaching the development of others, they experience psychophysiological effects that restore the body's natural healing and growth processes, thus enhancing their sustainability. We thus suggest that to sustain their effectiveness, leaders should emphasise coaching as a key part of their role and behavioural habits. Implications for future research on leadership and leadership development are discussed, as well as implications for the practice of leadership development and education."

Nathan Jamail, in his book, *The Leadership Playbook*, mentions that the greatest value of coaching is in giving the leader the ability to turn an idea into action.

According to ICF research, companies and organisations train their executives in coaching for the following reasons:

- to generate improved results
- to promote people's development
- to facilitate an improved working climate
- to create leadership standards
- to enhance the sustainability of
  - executives
  - companies and
  - society in general.

"To sustain their effectiveness, leaders should emphasise coaching as a key part of their role and behavioural habits."

— R. BOYATZIS, M. L. SMITH, AND N. BLAISE,
DEVELOPING SUSTAINABLE LEADERS THROUGH COACHING AND COMPASSION
ACADEMY OF MANAGEMENT LEARNING & EDUCATION, 2006, VOL. 5, NO. 1, 8–24.

4.1.4. The unique characteristics of the Coach Leader

Here, I present to you the main features that, in my opinion, distinguish the Coach Leader from any other leader.

THE COACH LEADER

"Although the coaching style may not scream 'bottom-line results,' it delivers them!"

— DR. DANIEL GOLEMAN, *DON'T WRITE OFF THE COACHING LEADERSHIP STYLE*, AUGUST 21, 2013, ARTICLE PUBLISHED ON LINKEDIN

A Coach Leader:

- inspires and co-creates visions with people, and thus increases commitment to them
- is genuinely interested in the personal development and well-being of people
- puts the common good above personal ambitions
- manages based on individual and group values
- offers and receives training constantly
- is balanced and has no repressed desires, restrictive beliefs, or prejudices, and, where such beliefs persist, works with another coach to achieve inner emancipation and improvement
- is trustworthy and humble without being hidden
- pursues constant personal development
- respects and understands the views of others
- assigns tasks and roles that are attractive and challenging to employees, leading them to discover their potential
- offers training and provides continuous and systematic constructive feedback
- systematically monitors the progress of the project
- helps people overcome obstacles to achieve their goals
- encourages and acknowledges every effort and motivates for better results

- has self-awareness, self-confidence, and balance
- according to Socrates, dares to explore and expose the truth
- according to Aristotle, seeks excellence by discovering and reaching their full potential, for themselves and the members of their team
- according to Plutarch, is a good role model for everyone
- according to Epictetus, has a resilient mindset
- has self-belief and faith in their team
- uses conflict for creative results
- acts proactively
- responds—does not react
- nurtures talent because everyone wants a challenging environment, even the top-performers
- motivates each one individually and all together
- acknowledges, rewards, and celebrates with the team.

It's a rather extended list, don't you think?

4.2. Coach Leader: lifestyle

Purpose

My purpose is to show you how a Coach Leader leads and what distinguishes them from other leaders.

The Coach Leader focuses on discovering the values of each person and the team they are called to lead or influence. I remind you that leadership is linked to influence.

I present two well-recognised and credible leadership models that, in my opinion, are the most effective. Then, I present the different ways a Coach Leader leads in relation to these two models. Finally, I make two suggestions: firstly, that we should strive to become role-model leaders, and secondly, that leadership courses should be introduced into the education system.

4.2.1. The main idea

First, I present the main idea behind the coaching leadership model with the help of two of the most classic and effective leadership models: **Tannenbaum and Schmidt** and **Hersey and Blanchard**. Then, I analyse the coaching leadership model, inviting you to adopt it in your daily practice of leadership. For the above two models, the choice of leadership behaviour depends on **external/internal conditions** and the **level of maturity of the people**. Many theorists, guru leaders, and experienced managers consider these parameters crucial for the choice of leadership style.

Tannenbaum and Schmidt

Tannenbaum and Schmidt propose a framework defined by two extremes. At the far left, leader-managers exercise fully their power over their subordinates and do not allow them the slightest degree of freedom or autonomy. Managers decide and order everything: what will happen, how it will happen, when it will happen, who will do it, etc. They do not allow the right to object, disagree, or express an opinion.

At the other end is the completely empowering style. Managers essentially delegate all their power to the subordinates and leave room for freedom of thought and action.

The authors describe the following representative leadership styles that are commonly encountered in practice:

ORDERS: The leader decides and announces it to the subordinates for execution.

PERSUADES: The leader decides and tries to convince the subordinates on the decision.

DISCUSSES: The leader presents the decisions and then invites questions and discusses obstacles or ways of implementation.

TRIES: The leader proposes decisions, which can be modified, after discussion with the subordinates.

CONSULTS: The leader first presents the problem, then gathers suggestions and opinions and, after careful consideration, decides.

ASKS PARTICIPATION: The leader explains the problem, defines the parameters, and asks the subordinates to co-decide.

DELEGATES–EMPOWERS: The leader allows subordinates to act as they see fit within the framework set by the superiors or the organisation.

Hersey and Blanchard: situational leadership

According to **Hersey and Blanchard's situational leadership model**, the most important parameter in choosing the appropriate leadership style is the level of development/maturity of the subordinates. The level of development is defined as a combination of their ability, knowledge, skills (I can), and willingness (I want) to achieve the goal.

Leadership style

- **S1: Directing/Telling Leaders**: The leader defines the roles and tasks of the subordinates and supervises (controls) them closely. Decisions are made and announced by the leader, so communication is one-way (**enthusiastic beginner**).
- **S2: Coaching (Selling Leaders)**: The leader defines the roles and tasks of the subordinates but also seeks out their opinion. Decisions are made by the leader, but there is two-way communication (**frustrated apprentice**).
- **S3: Supporting/Participating Leaders**: The leader delegates the daily decisions, such as assigning tasks and procedures, to the subordinates. The leader facilitates and takes part in the decisions, but the control remains with the subordinate (**hesitant partner**).
- **S4: Delegating Leaders**: The leader assigns responsibilities but also participates in decision making and problem solving. The control remains with the subordinates. Subordinates decide when and how the leader will participate (**autonomous, effective partner**).

4.2.2. Coaching leadership model

We have thoroughly defined the coach and the Coach Leader, and it becomes clear that there are **three things** that set Coach Leaders apart from any other leader.

They are primarily interested in people's **holistic growth** and are motivated by a **higher purpose** beyond personal ambitions, in a way that promotes the **responsibility and autonomy of the people**.

In other words, leaders act as a **moral compass** promoting a vision for a sustainable future. Their **existential orientation** is social eudaimonia and a fulfilled life.

This presupposes that they believe in people and constantly strive to develop them and bring out their best selves. They have a holistic approach to people development.

Holistic approach

A holistic approach to growth means that the aim is to develop the coachee—not only as a professional but also as a person.

People development through coaching involves **mind, soul, and heart**.

Coach Leaders pursue balance and happiness through self-actualisation and the use of potential in an ethical and sustainable way.

> Coach Leaders first become "excellent" leaders of themselves and then develop future Coach Leaders.

> MAIN IDEA
>
> Coach Leaders are leaders that remain coaches in every situation. They practice coaching every day, no matter the external or internal conditions or maturity level of the subordinates.
>
> Regardless of their leadership style, they always practice coaching.

Whichever leadership style you choose depending on the circumstances and characteristics of your team, you will always be a coach.

Coaching is the culture and mentality that guides your behaviour and decisions. It is not an occasional behaviour used in the spur of the moment. **It is a way of life** that affects you and your environment. A moral and authentic influence. A culture exemplified by your behaviour.

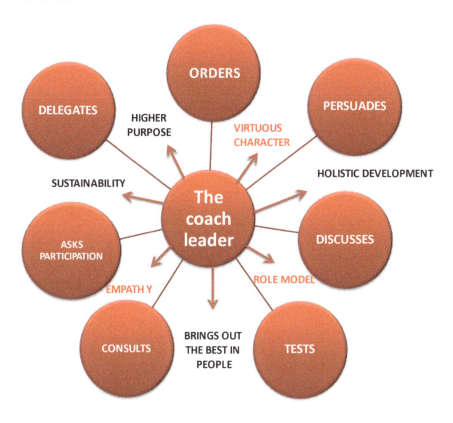

FIGURE 4.2.2. (A) THE CHARACTERISTICS OF THE COACH LEADER

In Figure 4.2.2. (a) the Coach Leader is at the core of and coexists with every leadership style. In this figure, **Tannenbaum and Schmidt's** leadership styles surround the Coach Leader. Hersey and Blanchard's leadership styles could be arranged in the same way, but I have not included them here.

In Figure 4.2.2. (b) we see the Coach Leader's path to achieving their ultimate goal.

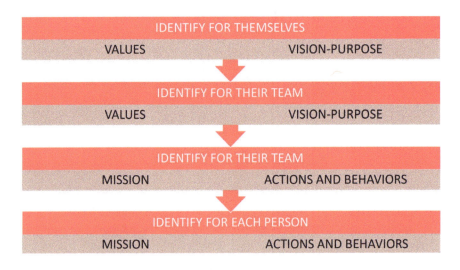

FIGURE 4.2.2. (B) THE COACH LEADER'S PATH TO SUCCESS

The Coach Leader's path

1. They identify their personal values and vision.
2. They establish the values of the team members and co-create the team values and vision.
3. They define the necessary actions and responsibilities and, finally, delegate them to each person according to their willingness and abilities.

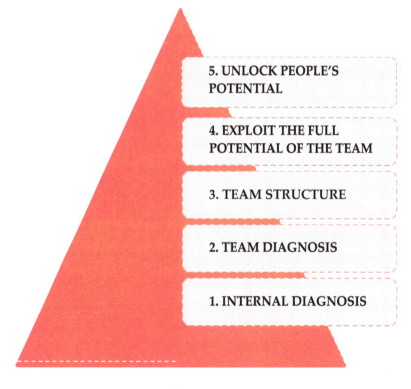

FIGURE 4.2.2. (C) THE COACH LEADER'S PATH

In Figure 4.2.2. (c), you see the stages Coach Leaders must go through to achieve their goals:

1. Inner enlightenment: revelation, self-knowledge (skills–abilities–values–vision).
2. Team enlightenment: revelation, self-knowledge (skills–abilities–values–vision).
3. Designing the group structure: functions, organisation, job analysis, job description, projects, goals.
4. Distributing team members to the projects, the right person to the right place; human resources management.
5. Human development.

4.2.3. The Coach Leader as a role model

According to **Richard Barrett** and his book, *The New Leadership Paradigm*, Coach Leaders practice the following:

- **Personal development coaching**: help team members deal with any internal obstacles that hinder their development
- **Professional development coaching**: help team members deal with business issues that hinder their growth
- **Efficiency coaching**: help team members achieve performance goals by teaching them to manage their resources more effectively and by making them responsible for their choices.

According to **Sir John Whitmore**, one of the pioneering coaching gurus, coaching is more than just a predetermined technique or methodology. It is a way of managing people and resources, a way of thinking, a way of life. Coaching requires the highest qualities: **empathy**, **integrity**, **detachment**, and, above all, a willingness to adopt a new, differentiated approach to human behaviour.

According to Richard Barrett, there are three key points that differentiate Coach Leaders from other leaders.

They help team members as follows:

1. **Facilitate** the creation of conscious awareness through interpreting with all senses.
2. **Foster** responsibility and initiative in all team members.
3. **Develop** the self-esteem and self-confidence of all team members.

According to **Marshall Goldsmith**, there are three key values that differentiate leaders who make a positive difference: courage, humility, and discipline. Moreover, they must earn credibility twice: first, they must be deemed competent, then they must be recognised for it.

Finally, I would like to remind you of the most important skills of the Coach Leader to confirm that coaching leadership is always applied:

- powerful questioning
- active listening
- complete understanding
- expanding perspective
- enhancing accountability.

Coach Leader training

If you wish to change your organisation, your company, or your team, you must first change the leaders.

Your goal is to transform every leader into a Coach Leader. But how?

By training them in coaching but also offering them personal coaching sessions.

Coach the Leader: The change in mentality cannot be achieved only through training. It should be combined with coaching sessions that require personal commitment and time investment!

4.2.4. Coaching leadership in education

I invite you to consider the benefits we would have if coaching leadership courses were part of our education system, from elementary school to university, for teachers and students alike! Would it make a difference?

Imagine the social skills our children would acquire and the impact on their future as people, professionals, and responsible citizens, equipped with the values and virtues of self-knowledge, justice, practical wisdom, prudence, justice, responsibility, bravery, vision for a higher purpose, and respect and support for the growth and self-actualisation of others.

Our children would be happier.

What do you think?

Leadership begins with leading oneself. This is the central message I want to convey through this book.

Inner leadership is a necessary condition to lead other people.

Each one of us is a potential leader, prioritising leadership of ourselves.

This path is a laborious inner journey that requires preparation and guidance, especially for younger people. It requires training and coaching sessions. The education system and teachers play an important role in this process.

Socrates was constantly trying to convince his environment to invest in education through his dialogues, but he was never funded by his students. Aristophanes was tragically unjust, accusing him of the opposite in his comedies (the devastating effects of populism led to the death of the most wise and ethical person in human history).

Socrates, throughout his life, exemplified his belief that **knowledge is the greatest good**, as necessary for our survival as the air we breathe.

Socrates argued that knowledge is the greatest of all other goods—more so than a beautiful body, wealth, or glory—because right knowledge is a prerequisite to properly manage these goods. Only when we know the true value of these goods can we manage them in a way that adds value to our life and the lives of others.

According to **Aristotle**, personal practice in self-control, combined with the decisive contribution of education, leads to an attitude of life (*hexis*) that allows us to subdue extreme desires and passions and use virtues as an ideal standard.

In **Plato**'s *The Republic*, virtue is instilled in citizens through education.

In all three great teachers, we see how important education is in shaping people's character through the knowledge and practice of virtues.

> Great teachers make great students; great coaches make great people and leaders.

Who is best suited to instil a love of learning in young people? The coach, especially the Coach Leader.

What would Alexander the Great be without Aristotle?

What would Plato be without Socrates, Aristotle without Plato?

Think about a teacher that lingers in your memory to this day. What was their most important trait?

Do you feel lucky to have met them?

What would have happened if you had never crossed paths?

4.2.5. The main points of the Coach Leader

Coach Leaders, as we saw, are different from other leaders because they are a moral compass of personal and social change toward a higher purpose that transcends personal ambitions. They are guided by an existential orientation for a meaningful life and inspire every person they meet.

Whatever leadership model they implement, they remain coaches, in every situation. They possess self-knowledge and practice the skills of the modern professional coach. They develop people by bringing to light their truth and hidden potential, as Socrates did 2500 years ago with his dialectical method.

Coach Leaders tap into the best self of the people around them, either in their personal lives or in their work. Self-awareness is a prerequisite for this great work.

Coach Leaders use the **Philosophership™** model in their day-to-day leadership. They first discover their own core values, then they discover the values of the people around them. Values act as a motivator and guide. They then co-create an existential orientation and attractive vision considering philosophy, and especially classical philosophy.

In their day-to-day leadership, they use the skills of a professional coach, as defined by the ICF, within an ethical framework that combines classical virtues and the ICF Code of Ethics, which binds all professional members.

Coach Leaders use coaching because it is the only modern process and tool that can sculpt leaders in an authentic way, according to their own abilities and aspirations.

In addition, coaching ensures the change in people's mentality and behaviour that is necessary to manage the current uncertain and complex conditions and attain personal and social happiness, prosperity, and sustainability.

> Coaching leadership is not just a leadership style—it is a lifestyle that affects you and your environment. It is an ethical and authentic influence, a culture that you can exemplify through your behaviour.

"Our mission in life is to make a positive difference, not to prove how smart or right we are."

— PETER F. DRUCKER

POINTS TO REMEMBER FROM STEP 4

- Leadership through coaching is not just another leadership model but a way of life.
- The Coach Leader is the combination of a trained coach and a visionary leader who inspires others and is inspired by common good above personal ambitions.
- Coaching leadership is adopted by more and more companies and organisations in the global private and public sectors due to the great and mutual value that is created.

- The Coach Leader puts the common goal above personal ambitions.
- The Coach Leader practices moral and intellectual virtues.
- The Coach Leader lives a meaningful life and cultivates meaningful connections.
- The Coach Leader is a role model.

Coach Leaders develop future leaders not to follow in their footsteps but to step in them so hard that they will erase them. That is, they lead in their own unique way.

PHILOSOPHICAL LEADERSHIP

YOUR TURN

Immediate action I will take:

Are there any obstacles? If so, what are they?

How will I overcome each obstacle?

STEP 5

THE FUNDAMENTAL SKILLS OF THE COACH LEADER

"The Coach Leader has unique skills, and the most dominant of these is effective communication, every day, by all possible means."

— BARBARA ASIMAKOPOULOU

PURPOSE

In the seventh step, I present some of the basic skills that the Coach Leader needs to possess. Effective communication is a key ability acquired through specific skills that I analyse in greater detail below.

5.1. Active listening

The purpose of active listening is to understand the feelings, thoughts, beliefs, needs, desires, and values of the speaker and assess their point of view, whether you agree with it or not.

Active listening, in essence, is the ability to fully concentrate on what your interlocutor is saying or not saying and to make it easier for them to express themselves by asking clarifying questions.

Tips for effective active listening:

- You may be tempted to give advice, but do not.
- Try not to judge their feelings as right or wrong. Just let them talk.
- Follow *their* agenda, not your own.
- Try to listen to their concerns, goals, beliefs, and desires without criticism.
- Read behind their words, tone of voice, and body language for any information that may be a source of inquiry.
- Do not get emotionally involved; try to remain detached, like the heroes in Brecht's plays. Listen with empathy without letting your emotions draw any conclusions.
- Be receptive to information and emotions.

> Hearing is one of the body's five senses, but listening is a skill.
>
> *The origin of this quote is unknown.*

What facilitates active listening?

- being fully concentrated on your interlocutor
- the mindfulness methodology
- emotional intelligence
- summarising to verify that you both understand each other
- encouragement and acceptance
- clear and concise clarifying questions
- allowing the coachee to clarify the situation without criticism
- maintaining eye contact
- attention to facial expressions
- observing the tone, volume, and rhythm of voice
- attention to body language
- emotional detachment
- non-distracting movements
- a quiet environment without distractions.

What impedes active listening?

- time pressure
- an unsuitable environment
- emotional charge
- selfishness/egocentrism
- arrogance
- restrictive beliefs and prejudices
- indifference

- concentration difficulties
- defensiveness
- lack of trust.

How to become a better listener

You can improve your listening skills by identifying the habits that distinguish effective listeners from ineffective ones.

Try not to be **self-centred** or **defensive**. You probably know a lot of people who have these annoying habits.

Egocentric listeners

Egocentric listeners take control of the conversation and talk for hours about themselves. They underestimate the concerns of others and act as if their own difficulties are twice as great.

Egocentric listeners are too preoccupied with themselves to listen and understand other people's experiences and feelings. Moreover, this attitude prevents them from discovering the real cause of the various challenges they face.

Defensive listeners

Defensive listeners take any comment as a personal attack. To protect themselves and their low self-esteem, they can distort your message by ignoring what does not confirm their view of themselves. By distorting the circumstances and the meaning, they miss the opportunity to find out what really happens in each case.

We are all occasionally guilty of egocentrism or defensiveness. It is a behaviour that we adopt when we are emotionally vulnerable.

In these cases, you need to make an extra effort to restrain yourself and not draw hasty conclusions or make any criticism.

Listening is selective

We usually listen and understand what we already have in mind. We choose what we listen to in a speech or a conversation. As a Coach Leader, you need to practice listening to what your interlocutor is really saying.

Some people are overly descriptive and embellish their speech with a lot of details that usually hide the essence. This can result in wasting valuable time or drawing false conclusions.

In this case, politely ask the interlocutor to focus on the essence of the matter to facilitate mutual awareness.

Use non-verbal skills, such as:

- maintaining eye contact
- reacting with head movements (nods)
- paying attention to the speaker's body language
- giving verbal cues, such as *I hear you, please continue,* etc.

What is the difference between active listening and passive listening?

Active listening is a process that promotes human development, and it requires effort on our part. Passive listening equates to hearing, which is one of the body's five senses. In active listening, you carefully pay attention to the speaker's words, body language, and feelings.

The benefits of active listening

Active listening helps you discover the value behind every conversation and bring to light things that are important for the coachees and the achievement of their goals.

> Hearing + Attention = Active Listening

An added benefit of active listening is that you are relieved of the pressure to have all the answers. By listening closely to the other person, you guide them to concentrate on themselves and on what they are saying. This way, they discover new things about themselves or confirm old discoveries.

By listening carefully, you avoid or prevent problems that may arise in an individual or a team.

5.2. The art of speech—effective use of language

Using a rich vocabulary and semantically or emotionally strong words in communication increases the influence of the writer or the speaker and motivates the reader and the listener, respectively.

> The right words can change a person's life.

The elements of appropriate language

An honest, clear language influences, seduces, persuades, and can bring about great change.

The elements of appropriate language are:

- choice of vocabulary, phrases, metaphors, stories
- alignment with the coachee's vocabulary and experience
- appropriate tone of voice, volume, rhythm, and expression
- time (i.e., duration and pauses).

In the end, it is the coachees who decide how these words influence their decisions and life and to what extent.

Ways to develop a rich vocabulary and effective written or spoken language:

- Always listen carefully.
- Read all kinds of literature.
- Listen and read the masters of oral and written speech through movies, plays, speeches, radio, audio books, blogs, articles, newspapers, etc. Here are some people you could follow: professor of strategic management Haridimos Tsoukas, author and philosopher Stelios Ramfos, byzantinologist Helene Ahrweiler, professor of philosophy Christos Yiannaras, journalist Paschos Mandravelis, and journalist and author Soti Triantafillou.
- Associate with people who are eloquent and know how to say the right thing at the right time in the right way.
- Attend speech and language development courses such as creative writing.
- Study dictionaries of synonyms and antonyms like the wonderful dictionary of Professor Georgios Babiniotis that I often reference.

- Listen to yourself speak. Record your speech and listen to it afterwards. Observe what you are doing well and what needs improving.
- Resist hackneyed phrases or repetitive words. Enrich your vocabulary.
- Practice oral and written speech, follow lectures, and write comments, articles, and books.
- Create your own blog or newsletter.

When speech becomes art

Speech becomes art when it involves the listeners in an authentic way and responds genuinely to their own way of perceiving things.

For example, when:

- it has rhythm
- it has structure, a beginning, and an end
- it includes beautiful, non-trite words that accurately express the message you want to convey
- it expresses and evokes emotions
- it illuminates and inspires the listener
- it is simple and clean
- less is more
- it has arguments and logic
- it includes stories with which the listener can identify
- it becomes narrative when needed.

According to Aristotle (Book II "Rhetoric."), the art of public speaking includes **ethos**, **pathos**, and **logos**—a character that inspires credibility (ethos), emotions that unite and magnetise (pathos), and, finally, essence, which is logic and arguments (logos).

It is in this section that Aristotle delves into the three modes of persuasion—ethos, pathos, and logos—and provides explanations and examples of each.

In "Rhetoric," Aristotle discusses various persuasive techniques and strategies for effective communication. The concepts of ethos, pathos, and logos are central to his understanding of rhetoric. Ethos refers to the speaker's credibility and ethical appeal, pathos refers to appealing to the emotions of the audience, and logos refers to logical reasoning and evidence.

In more detail:

Effective speakers who possess the art of speech win their audience as follows:

ETHOS

A character acquired through the practice of moral and intellectual virtues, according to Aristotle.

Moral virtues: honesty with oneself and others, authenticity, self-control, wisdom, bravery, temperance, generosity, meekness, kindness.

Intellectual virtues: "techne" (artistic or technical knowledge), "episteme" (scientific knowledge) "gnosis" (philosophic wisdom, philosophy), "wisdom" (practical wisdom), and "noesis" (judgement, perceptive ability).

Speakers who honour and express the above human qualities establish the necessary credibility and authenticity with their audience.

PATHOS

In order for the audience to be interested in a speech, they need to feel the speaker's love and authority on the topic and also to be emotionally involved.

Speakers who speak from the heart, and do not use only logic and arguments, exude positive energy and evoke emotions.

According to African American poet Maya Angelou, "People usually forget what you tell them, but they never forget how you made them feel."

LOGOS

A speech must be structured, thorough; it must contain arguments, evidence, examples, logical reasoning and, of course, meet the needs of the audience.

The external conditions and environment in which a speech takes place are also essential. The room should enhance the credibility and validity of the speaker, not weaken or challenge it.

5.3 The art of effective questioning

Asking powerful questions is one of the most important coaching skills (ICF Core Competency #7). The art of effective questioning is largely based on the **dialectical method of Socrates**.

Dialectic derives from the word "dialogue." Socrates engaged in philosophical dialogue and used a method of questioning to stimulate critical thinking and explore deeper understanding. Socrates used this argumentative form of dialogue to find the truth. He believed that genuine knowledge came from discovering universal definitions of the key concepts governing life, such as virtue, good, and evil.

Socrates taught by asking questions, drawing out answers from his interlocutors to challenge the completeness and accuracy of their thinking. The purpose was to make them think about the presuppositions and unquestioned beliefs on which their arguments were founded. Through simplistic examples, he showed the extreme consequences of these views, thus proving the fragility of their arguments.

He led his interlocutors to discover new conclusions and new approaches to the truth, which he believed to be within every human being.

To gain insights into the Dialectical Method of Socrates, it is beneficial to explore Plato's works, particularly those featuring Socratic dialogues. Plato's dialogues present conversations between Socrates and various interlocutors, showcasing Socrates' method of inquiry.

One notable dialogue that exemplifies the Dialectical Method is Plato's "Meno." In this dialogue, Socrates engages in a discussion with Meno about the nature of virtue and whether it can be taught. The dialogue illustrates Socrates' approach of asking probing questions to examine the interlocutor's beliefs and uncover inconsistencies or contradictions in their understanding.

Awareness through questions

Effective questioning is a step-by-step investigation of a subject to discover the truth, which leads to awareness. Awareness is internal knowledge about oneself or the environment that lights the way toward the achievement of one's goals.

For the Coach Leader, the purpose of questions is to help the coach understand the coachee. This knowledge works as a catalyst for coachees to grow and utilise their skills. I will remind you here that, according to Aristotle, eudaimonia is fulfilling your potential. We conclude, then, that **awareness is a prerequisite for eudaimonia**.

Effective questions possess the following characteristics:

- they are formed in language the coachee understands
- they enable self-discovery by the coachee
- they aim at discovery
- they do not affect the answer
- they showcase active listening
- they are penetrating
- they create clarity
- they move the coachee forward
- they improve the coachee
- they show the way towards the achievement of their goal
- they are open-ended
- they are asked one at a time
- they are non-directional
- they are positive
- they are targeted
- they are exploratory

- they are related to what the coachee wants to discover
- they are not threatening
- they are non-judgmental.

Basic types of questions are designed to:

- identify the feeling
- investigate what is happening in the present
- help the coachees understand more about themselves
- be investigative
- be thought-provoking
- be informative
- explore alternative views
- seek orientation
- presuppose integrity
- facilitate goal setting
- encourage talking and actions
- look for solutions
- motivate
- activate
- be powerful
- lead to solutions and a plan of action
- reveal how the coachee can change a situation.

5.4. Message transmission

A message is anything that the coach shares with the coachees concerning a reality, a principle, or a point of view to help them better understand, achieve their goals, and grow.

In the coaching relationship, it is important to take into consideration the coachee's mindset, expectations, and goals. The message should be focused on the receiver. Each message needs to be fully personalised to be immediately understood by the coachee.

Messages fall into two broad categories:

1. Informational messages designed to
    - **inform**, providing information that is generally accepted and enlightens the coachee
    - share **personal experience**, such as a personal story that helps the coachee understand another point of view
    - **connect**, making the connection between different thoughts, in order for an important truth to emerge
    - express **understanding with genuine interest**—you should always express your understanding of what the coachee has said, done or not done, even if you have a different opinion.

2. Encouraging messages designed to
    - **encourage**—the coach plays an important role in the coachee's commitment to accomplish what is for their benefit
    - **motivate**, encouraging the coachee and expressing confidence in their capabilities
    - **call for action**, asking the coachee to take specific actions that lead them closer to their goals
    - show **respect**—a coaching relationship is based on mutual respect that cultivates trust, a necessary background for creative thoughts and actions
    - show **evidence** to ascertain the progress of the coachee.

5.5. Acknowledgment

Coaches build the coachee's self-confidence and self-esteem, encourage them to overcome obstacles, and acknowledge every micro step toward the achievement of their goals.

The process of acknowledgment includes the following steps:

Applaud

Coaches pay attention to every step their coachees take, applauding the effort and any result.

Sport players are applauded by the fans for every good effort throughout the game, even if they lose. It is fuel for them to keep trying.

When you persistently continue the effort, you have a chance of achieving the goal.

Focus on strengths

Usually, people focus on their shortcomings and weaknesses. Coaches focus on strengths and build on them when determining the next steps and improvements.

Coaching enhances people's self-esteem and self-confidence, which are essential throughout the process of growth.

Establish expectations

Coachees should feel like you are an ally and supporter every step of the way. That way, you can ask from them more than they ask from themselves.

Example: "I expect you to bring [this result] next week. What do you think?"

In this way, you show them the potential for improvement. They will either respond to the challenge positively or present obstacles. You can then talk about how they will overcome these obstacles.

5.6. Obstacles

There will always be obstacles, internal or external, for every thought or action. Some of the internal barriers are prejudice, low self-esteem, avoidance of responsibility, procrastination, fear of not being liked, fear of failure, etc. The coach's role is to help the coachee perceive each obstacle and gradually overcome it. The same is true for external obstacles. In case they cannot be influenced, the coachee should accept the external conditions and proceed accordingly.

5.7. Directness

Experienced coaches are direct and honest, and they do not manipulate the coachees. They inspire and encourage them to act. It is the coachee's responsibility to decide and assume the consequences. Coaches express in a positive way every thought or opinion that can give more information to the coachees and help them gain awareness.

5.8. Vision

Coaches evoke the vision they have created with the coachee at every opportunity. It is the purpose that makes the steps easier to achieve. A motivational vision is a great way for the coachee to get back on track, overcome obstacles, and move on.

5.9. The role of silence

Silence is a tool used by the skilled coach to create space for the coachee to think, express, and liberate.

Negative emotions such as fear, are, many times, suppressed in the back of our minds, and we refuse to admit them even to ourselves. Through silence, coaches create the right conditions for exploration and discovery.

Silence can be a source of embarrassment for some; however, for effective listeners, it creates mutual value.

Silence is discovery.

Silence is respect.

Silence is a virtue.

Silence creates value.

Fewer words on the part of the coach leave the necessary time and space to the coachee. The suggested coachee–coach speech ratio is 80/20, respectively.

5.10. Celebration

Celebrating a result, an achievement, a successful endeavour, or any significant effort is essential in the coaching process. It closes a circle, creates relief, and paves the way for a new cycle.

Celebrations are inextricably linked to the culture of each people and serve multiple purposes—one of which is the expression of gratitude for what we already have. Moreover, it gives impetus for new beginnings and new efforts.

5.11. Creative conflict resolution

The role of the Coach Leader is to prevent conflicts. However, in any work or social environment, conflicts are often inevitable. The Coach Leader needs to resolve creatively any conflict that lurks or eventually occurs.

Definition
Conflict is a dispute caused by competing interests or personality differences between individuals, individuals and groups, or different groups.

Every conflict is an opportunity for a creative outcome

Although conflict involves risk, the Coach Leader does not shy away from it because, if there is no longer a common goal, rupture is also a solution. If there is still a common purpose, conflict is creative and results in finding new ways of communication. Non-creative conflict is catastrophic for any social system.

Our goal, therefore, is to anticipate and resolve any form of conflict creatively.

Conflict resolution benefits

When a conflict is resolved, we feel safe. We trust the other party, and we communicate better. When there is no trust, conversely, there is no communication. We do not feel safe; we feel threatened—and a conflict is possible.

Trust is a prerequisite for effective communication.

> Conflict is the symptom of a problem, and problems must be resolved.

In times of crisis, feelings of insecurity and anxiety (negative emotions) about the future prevail. In this case, cultivating trust is the Coach Leader's primary concern. Trust improves communication. And when there is communication, adaptation to the new conditions or, even better, acceptance of the new conditions is possible.

Effective communication facilitates collaboration, increases satisfaction, and leads to happy people.

CREATIVE CONFLICT RESOLUTION PROCESS

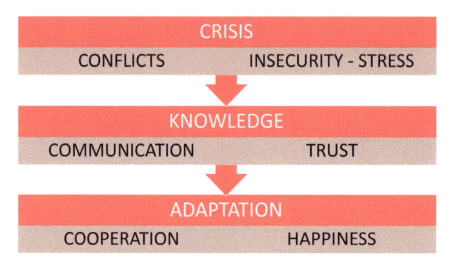

FIGURE 5.11. CREATIVE CONFLICT RESOLUTION AND ACHIEVEMENT OF COOPERATION

Figure 5.11: shows the process of creative conflict resolution to achieve cooperation.

Ways to predict a conflict

Transparency and clear instructions from the start prevent miscommunication and misunderstanding.

Information, knowledge, effective message delivery, and feedback facilitate communication and prevent a potential conflict. It has been shown that most conflicts occur due to ineffective communication. Having a commonly accepted purpose and being reminded of it whenever conflict arises is crucial. Feedback, perspective feedback, positive reframing, and NLP (neuro-linguistic programming) are all essential elements.

Instructions for conflict mediation

- Take a **neutral position** and treat both parties in the same way.
- Determine if the conflict is rooted in **work structure** or people's **personalities**.
- Explain why it is necessary to resolve the conflict.
- Ask everyone to express their opinion on the problem.
- Ask everyone to repeat each other's point of view on the problem.
- Ask every party to speak on behalf of the other.
- Ask everyone to talk about each other's positive traits.
- Always ask everyone to confirm the accuracy of their point of view when repeated by the other party.
- Once the problem has been clarified, always focus your attention on the objective facts of the situation. By clarifying the problem, you do not allow anyone to comment or express opinions about what the other person mentioned before.
- Where possible, try to help people discover common needs or goals.
- Try to make sure that the **solution emerges from the participants** themselves.
- When the facts become clear, ask everyone to suggest a solution.
- Lead the two parties to agree on specific steps that will resolve the conflict.
- Always set a date to review the progress of the solution.

Listed below are four problem-solving criteria as formulated by **Fisher and Ury** in their book, *Getting to Yes*. The interlocutors work together to solve the problem. The purpose is a prudent result reached in a positive and friendly way.

1. Separate people from the problem.
2. Focus on the interests, not the positions.
3. Invent a set of options aimed at mutual benefit.
4. Insist on the use of objective criteria.

Conflict resolution strategies

As a leader, you will face conflicts between people in your team, but there will also be times when you are in conflict with a partner, employee, customer, or supplier.

According to **Kenneth W. Thomas** and **Ralph H. Kilmann** and the managerial grid model of **Robert R. Blake** and **Jane Mouton**, there are five conflict strategies that combine the satisfaction of your own interests with those of the other person.

These strategies are:

Avoidance This way of handling conflict overlooks the interests of the conflicting parties, resorts to indirect means, or postpones reporting on the issues at stake. This is an effective strategy in cases of minor conflicts (e.g., that are forgotten over time).

Adjustment/Settlement This way of handling conflict means neglecting one's interests in order to win the other side over. It is chosen by people who want to preserve personal relationships. This is an effective way to proceed if what one party loses is less significant than what the other party will lose.

Competition This way of dealing with a conflict is an attempt to achieve one's goals by harming or defeating the other party—for example, through arguments, threats, show of force, or physical violence. This strategy is effective when immediate decision and action is required.

Compromise This way of handling conflict seeks partial satisfaction for both parties through a middle ground that involves some sacrifice on both sides. It is applied when there is a lack of time and will. In this case, both parties will probably lose something.

Collaboration This way of handling conflict provides a mutually accepted solution to a problem. The parties inform each other about their respective goals and then work to achieve a mutually beneficial solution. This is the best way to resolve a conflict, especially when there is time and maturity on both sides.

According to professors **Kenneth Cloke** and **Joan Goldsmith**, in their book *Workplace Conflict Resolution: 10 Strategies for All*, to cope with and effectively resolve a workplace conflict, we must adopt the following strategies:

1. Understand the culture and dynamics of the conflict.
2. Listen with empathy and feedback.
3. Look for hidden messages below the surface.
4. Identify and reframe the emotions.
5. Separate the important from what stands in the way.
6. Prepare mentally for creative problem-solving.

7. Attach great importance to defining the problem.
8. Lead and advise in order to transform.
9. Explore resistance and negotiate collaboratively.
10. Design prevention systems and use mediation.

In all models of conflict resolution, the presence of a coach or a Coach Leader is crucial during the whole process.

5.12. Effective communication techniques

5.12.1. Reframing

Reframing is a communication technique derived from Cognitive Behavioural Therapy (CBT). It is also known as "cognitive restructuring," but, in my opinion, "reframing" is a much better term.

The technique of reframing involves identifying and then challenging irrational or negative thoughts, and finally interpreting the facts themselves with a positive approach.

Reframing is a way of projecting facts, experiences, ideas, concepts, and feelings to find more positive alternative solutions. I would call it a more well-intentioned look at the matter. Reframing can occur either voluntarily or automatically in all cases.

Example:

My boss is constantly checking on me. He does not trust me.

How can we interpret this matter positively using the reframing technique?

Considering the same matter from a positive angle, what would you think about the specific behaviour of your boss?

Could it be that they trust you and invest time in your training?

5.12.2. Feedback and feedforward

Feedback

Feedback is the presentation and evaluation of ideas, thoughts, actions, situations, and behaviours that occurred in the past.

Usually, someone who gives feedback describes something that has happened in the past according to their own perception, which may differ from other people's perception.

As we have seen in a previous step, people perceive reality differently. Although it is subjective, feedback is useful to see what actions and decisions need to be taken next.

Due to its subjective nature, it is better to obtain feedback from various sources to increase its reliability.

Examples of feedback tools:

- employee performance appraisal systems
- psychometric tests
- employee satisfaction and opinion surveys.

The executive or consultant who is called to interpret the results of the above tools should recognise the value of consistent feedback but also its limited effectiveness in creating change if it is not combined with feedforward.

Feedforward

Feedforward is the presentation of ideas, thoughts, and actions that are intended to improve a situation or behaviour. According to **Marshall Goldsmith**, the #1 leadership and coaching guru, feedforward can, for the most part, replace feedback and give better results.

The main argument behind this statement is that focusing on the past does not work because the past cannot be changed. Our behaviour changes only with ideas and ways that can be applied in the future. I suggest you practice feedforward by asking the team to give their own improvement ideas for each person separately, including you, the Coach Leader.

Attachment to past behaviours is not helpful. It is a source of grievances, and it hampers improvement in the future. The past gives us useful information to take action in the present and future, but we should not fall prey to useless criticism, a behaviour that consumes mental and spiritual energy.

5.12.3. Summarising

Summarising is a powerful communication tool that enhances awareness. Whether it is done by the coachee or the coach, with the permission of the coachee, it provides the opportunity to clarify the message and gain a common understanding.

Personally, I find it useful for the coachee, during and at the end of a coaching conversation, to summarise the main points of the awareness they have gained so far.

As for the coach, I suggest summarising often, especially when you need to clarify something or bring the conversation back to the original mutually agreed purpose. It also helps the coachee clarify their thoughts, choices, or desired actions.

By summarising, the coach confirms whether the coaching conversation is on the right track or the original goal needs to be redefined with the coachee.

POINTS TO REMEMBER FROM STEP 5

- Coach Leaders lead their team forward in a genuine way.
- Coach Leaders are a catalyst for creative change and solving complexity.
- Coach Leaders develop people.
- Coach Leaders create new leaders.
- Coach Leaders are constantly evolving.
- The skills that distinguish the Coach Leader are effective communication, powerful questioning, creative conflict resolution, vision, acknowledgment, celebration, and the art of speech.

YOUR TURN

Immediate action I will take:

Are there any obstacles? If so, what are they?

How will I overcome each obstacle?

STEP 6

COACHING LEADERSHIP: VALUES-BASED LEADERSHIP

"The main task of the Coach Leader is to activate the will (values) and cultivate the practice of moral and intellectual virtues for personal and social well-being."

— BARBARA ASIMAKOPOULOU

PURPOSE

The purpose of the eighth step is to introduce the Coach Leader's ultimate tool for activating people in the practice of everyday leadership: **values** and **virtues**.

The theory of values highlights the importance of uncovering people's personal and common group values and cultivating a favourable environment for their expression.

My purpose is to reinforce the modern theory of values with Ancient Greek virtues as the necessary human qualities to facilitate their expression.

In the first subsection, I present the Ancient Greek aretalogy, the science of the virtues, (*aretes*, in Greek) and, mainly, the moral and intellectual virtues of Aristotle.

In the second subsection, I delve into the great power of values as a source of motivation, inspiration, orientation, and commitment to a higher purpose: personal and social eudaimonia.

In the third subsection, I introduce the concept of existential orientation through Ancient Greek philosophy and the school of existential psychotherapy represented by great psychotherapists such as **May** and **Yalom**.

6.1. Aretology—the path to eudaimonia

The modern Coach Leader takes into account the motivation theories of modern psychologists such as **Maslow, Herzenberg, Argyris, Vroom**, and **Goleman**. They also consider the most up-to-date value theories presented by **Coach University**, the pioneering international educational organisation; Professor of Athens University of Economics and Business **Dimitris Bourantas**; British Executive Coach **Richard Barrett**; and #1 Executive Coach and Leadership Thinker, Dr. **Marshall Goldsmith**.

The modern theory of values as motives is an extension of the Ancient Greek aretalogy—that is, the teaching of virtues in the age of **Socrates** and **Plato**, and especially on the moral and intellectual virtues of **Aristotle**, which I presented extensively in the third step.

6.1.1. Socrates, virtues, and the art of living

Virtues, before the time of Socrates and Plato, represented the social quality of a person and their ability to perform certain tasks correctly in order to succeed in life.

However, the origin of aretalogy as a science is attributed to Socrates, who according to his student Plato, ascribes to virtues a broader moral meaning. He highlights the value of virtues as **moral standards for optimal living**.

For this reason, Aristotle considered Socrates a scientist of ethics and a teacher of the art of living.

6.1.2. The soul as a source of energy and motivation

According to Plato and Aristotle, the soul is much more than we might believe. Plato argues that **the soul's health depends on virtue**. I believe that this means that the individual who practices virtues has a serene and contented soul.

Vassilis Kalfas, professor of philosophy at the Aristotle University of Thessaloniki, in his book, *Aristotle, Behind the Philosopher*, states that the Aristotelian soul is the "form" of the natural body that maintains an inseparable relationship with it. It is expressed by the pair of concepts "energy" (soul) and "power" (body). That is, the soul is the realisation of the body's ability to live.

In conclusion, only if we have a fulfilled and satisfied soul can we live.

Aristotle argues that the soul is what gives us the energy and motivation for survival, development, thought, and intellect. He further develops the idea of the soul.

The soul is behind our every action, according to Aristotle.

He, like Plato, believes that the soul is expressed through virtues.

In the third step, I presented the moral and intellectual virtues of Aristotle as the good (ideal) qualities of the soul of every human being. I also presented their corresponding excess and deficiency. By avoiding bad (destructive) qualities, you follow an ideal model of behaviour that leads to a happy and fulfilling life. Thus, according to Aristotle, the reward for practicing the good qualities of the soul is eudaimonia.

Virtues such as justice, liberality (generosity), and magnanimity are qualities of people who have a positive contribution to society. Their excess or deficiency, such as injustice, avarice, and pettiness, are the bad qualities of the soul.

Aristotle addresses the nature of the soul in some of his writings. His most comprehensive treatment of the subject can be found in his work titled "On the Soul." This consists of three books and explores Aristotle's philosophical inquiry into the nature and functions of the soul.

According to **Aristotle**, those who practice moral and intellectual virtues acquire good habits and have a balanced and serene soul. Every virtue represents the supremacy of the soul, while every excess or deficiency exemplifies the adventures of the soul.

In conclusion, good, praiseworthy deeds originate from virtues and bad, sinful deeds originate from their excess or deficiency.

Universal citizen

Aristotle puts forward the principles of the universal citizen. The universal human being lives in different parts of the world. Thus, Aristotle masterfully addresses the arrogance of native Athenians. (The birthplace of Aristotle was Stagira of northern Greece, not Athens, to which he moved when he was in his twenties. He was never an Athenian citizen). These principles are the virtues that function as standards for the performance evaluation of human actions.

While Aristotle does touch upon the concept of citizenship and political community in his writings, his focus is primarily on the city-state (polis) as the fundamental unit of political organisation.

Aristotle's most notable work on politics is "Politics," where he explores various aspects of governance, forms of government, and the role of citizens within the city-state.

Aristotle sought to understand the natural world, the cosmos, human beings, and their place in the universe. His interdisciplinary approach combined philosophy, observation, and systematic inquiry, setting the stage for the development of scientific methods in later centuries.

The virtuous citizen chooses a moral behaviour based on "reason"— that is, logic and judgment (Nicomachean Ethics 1107 a1–2).

This is important! Aristotle, as a scientist, proposes logic and judgment that require observation, research, and argument as criteria for our choices. He warns us against making choices based only on emotions.

The virtuous individual uses **judgment** and critical thinking to choose the appropriate behaviour for a balanced, happy life. Judgment is included in the virtue of wisdom, the greatest virtue proposed by both Socrates and Aristotle. I refer to the great virtue of wisdom more below.

The Stoic philosophers expanded on Aristotle's theory of virtues, highlighting the importance of the divine and especially nature as points of reference and conditions of perfection.

According to Thomas Aquinas, an Italian philosopher and theologian with significant influence on Western thought and forerunner of Christian Aristotelianism, a person's virtues, as well as their vices, are in fact habits for which they are absolutely responsible.

6.1.3. Practical wisdom (phronesis)—the highest virtue

According to Professor **Vassilis Kalfas**, Aristotle seems to believe in the necessity of setting objective and absolute moral rules. His ethics are focused on highlighting an ideal type of person—the "wise"—who is the role model and the measure of moral behaviour. Therefore, the **highest virtue of every responsible citizen is wisdom**.

Wisdom is the intellectual virtue that consists of the individual's ability to distinguish right from wrong, good from evil. It is the sensible assessment of each circumstance. Practical wisdom is the result of valid knowledge (science) and human experience (practice).

Aristotelian wisdom is reminiscent of the Delphic maxim inscribed in the forecourt of the Temple of Apollo at Delphi, "nothing in excess" and, at the same time, the Socratic art of living.

The practice of wisdom, therefore, directs human behaviour to identify the right measure in every situation and offers a yardstick for correct life orientation.

Finally, it facilitates the outline of an existential orientation, represented by the existential psychotherapy of Yalom and May, as well as the modern science and art of coaching.

6.1.4. Habit and addiction, according to Aristotle

The dominant tendency that characterises Aristotle's analysis for the perception and creation of knowledge is empiricism (i.e., the coordination of the five senses). The intellect (passive and poetic mind) will be of particular concern to later Aristotelian philosophy.

According to Aristotle, virtues are acquired through habit and addiction—that is, through daily practice.

"Moral virtues are not introduced to the human soul by the outside, by the knowledge or teaching of the moral code. They require the repeated practice of the illogical part of the soul according to the requirements of the logical part." (*Nicomachean Ethics*)

Therefore, the main responsibility for the acquisition of moral virtues lies with individuals themselves. It requires the activation of will and cultivation of perseverance to repeatedly practice good deeds.

It is the Coach Leader's responsibility to discover and activate the will for themselves and their team and, therefore, cultivate perseverance in the daily practice of virtues.

6.1.5. Aristotle—art and science

Aristotle is both a researcher and a founder of science with the purpose of facilitating people's lives. He provides reliable and scientifically valid answers to life's questions based on research and observation of the nature. Aristotle considers research and knowledge as a means to a better life, and not as an end in itself.

Aristotle is recognised as one of the most influential scientists in history such as much as philosopher. His contributions to various fields of study, including biology, zoology, physics, and metaphysics, were groundbreaking during his time and continued to shape Western thought for centuries.

Aristotle approached scientific inquiry through empirical observation and classification. He believed that understanding the natural world required careful observation and analysis of the characteristics, behaviours, and functions of living organisms and objects. Aristotle's scientific methodology involved detailed descriptions, classification of species, and the identification of causes and purposes.

In his work "Physics," Aristotle investigated the principles and causes of natural phenomena. He explored concepts such as motion, time, space, and the nature of elements. While some of his conclusions may not align with modern scientific understanding, Aristotle's approach to studying the physical world and his emphasis on causation and observation were influential in the development of scientific thought.

While some of Aristotle's scientific theories have been refined or replaced by subsequent discoveries, his methodological approach and emphasis on empirical observation laid the groundwork for the scientific investigations that followed, making him an important figure in the history of science.

6.1.6. Every citizen is a social and political being

A virtuous citizen is defined first and foremost by their will to engage in civic activities. According to Aristotle, there is no righteousness outside the social and political life.

Isolation is not a desirable situation; on the contrary, it is a source of suffering. In this sense, a human is defined by Aristotle as a political being.

It is not easy for an isolated person to remain active. Activation is more likely when we coexist with others. According to Aristotle, the development of social life is analogous to the development of nature and the biological development of species. This reminds us that **nature is a great source of knowledge.**

The statement that "human is a social animal" is attributed to Aristotle. This idea can be found in his work "Politics." In Book I, Chapter 2 of "Politics," Aristotle discusses the nature of human beings and their inclination towards sociality. He argues that humans have a natural tendency to live in communities and form social bonds, engaging in social interactions and participating in political life.

Distinguishing them from other animals.

It underscores the importance of communal life, cooperation, and the pursuit of the common good within the context of human flourishing.

Moreover, Socrates, through his dialogues, teaches us that self-knowledge and improvement are achieved through interaction with other people and not through isolation.

Socrates' and Aristotle's views on human interaction as a prerequisite for improvement and development confirm that the coach is a crucial component of this process.

6.1.7. Freedom

According to Aristotle, free citizens have the ability to govern and be governed, to live as they wish, and not be determined by others (*Politics* 1317 b12).

Free individuals, however, **pursue happiness while respecting the institutions of the city**. A "good" life consists of a temperate and reasonable life that enables individuals to properly perform their social duties as responsible citizens and ensures they have the appreciation, friendship, and recognition of their peers.

6.1.8. Political leadership

Aristotle's political theory is governed by moderation and realism. His political system, especially in his later books (*Politics*), combines basic principles of democracy and aristocratic meritocracy.

It is closer to parliamentary democracy, since rulers must be elected, not drawn. This choice does not emanate from a belief in the equality of citizens but from **political realism**.

Aristotle considers democracy the least unjust of the regimes (monarchy, oligarchy). He argues, however, that **the average citizen needs to possess at least a molecule of wisdom** for the majority to be better than the few.

> According to Aristotle, the practice of moral and intellectual virtues and the love of nature, research, and knowledge are motivations for a meaningful life with breadth and depth; a life of magnanimity, enjoyment, gratitude, and forgiveness; a purposeful life in the pursuit of eudaimonia.

6.2. Values-based leadership

Aretalogy still finds modern devotees, some of whom refer to virtues as virtues and others as values.

In my opinion, the most coherent view on virtue is that of **Professor Seligman**, the father of positive psychology. He promotes virtues as the necessary human qualities for a happy, flourishing life. His virtues include those of Aristotle, as well as those put forward by later aretalogists, such as the Stoic philosopher **Epictetus** and the Roman emperor **Marcus Aurelius**.

Marcus Aurelius was one of the greatest Roman emperors and an important representative of Stoicism. In his wonderful book, *Meditations*, which I highly recommend, Marcus Aurelius gives answers to a multitude of questions and fears that plague people to this day, such as the fear of death.

Allow me to remind you that the aim of Coach Leaders is to achieve their personal purpose and, at the same time, develop their people toward a higher purpose, in alignment with their own values and the values of their team.

6.2.1. Modern definition of values

Personal values are **high aspirations, excluding material goods**, that are genuine and distinguish us from other people. If people have the opportunity to express them, they are satisfied and fulfilled.

They are authentic desires, as opposed to a conventional, socially defined framework of action. Otherwise, they would be limiting beliefs and obstacles to the natural evolution of every human being. Thus, if one of our values is security and the other adventure, there must be a conflict.

Our behaviours and actions arise from our true values.

People feel happy when they are in an environment where they can express their values.

Example: Think of a person whose value is creativity. If they have the opportunity to create, they will be happy. Otherwise, they will lack satisfaction and fulfilment.

Another value that I particularly appreciate is aesthetics. When a person appreciates elegance, beauty, and harmony, they literally suffer in a tasteless, unappealing environment.

From a young age, wherever I found myself, even for a brief time, I had the habit of cleaning, tidying, and decorating the space I was in. Some people consider it a waste of energy if it is just for a short stay. Obviously, in my hierarchy of values, aesthetics is much higher compared to other people. People who hold this value high do not think of it as a waste of time.

We will talk more in depth about values in the seventh step, where I introduce the Philosophership™ model. Values are the motivation and reference point that help a person set priorities and make appropriate decisions, with consistency and endurance to any internal or external obstacle. Here, I would like to expand more on the difference between **values** and **needs**.

Values are the motive behind any purposeful action. Needs are the means or expression of values, not the motive itself.

Behind every expressed need hides a value. Transportation is a necessity, but the rationale behind the vehicle's brand and appearance are personal values, such as safety, ostentation, luxury, or adventure.

I am sure that each of the above values brings to mind a different car; if people wanted to express the value of ostentation, they would buy a Porsche; if people wanted to express the value of adventure, they would choose a Jeep.

An entertaining game is to ask your team members to tell you what car they would buy if the conditions were ideal. Make sure you emphasise the term *ideal conditions*.

Attention: Usually, people are so affected by unfavourable conditions or limiting beliefs that they do not allow even a wish to pass through the filter of their mind. They stifle the desire before it even appears in the realm of fantasy. For optimal outcomes in this game aimed at identifying true values, help them dream and overcome the external obstacle of limited resources; help your team members free their minds of any internal or external obstacles and express themselves honestly. I guarantee that everyone will enjoy this process!

6.2.2. The role of the Coach Leader

The Coach Leader is called to uncover people's values—which, in many cases, are not clear and, in other cases, have not yet been expressed.

People usually express a need first (e.g., a house, a car). It is easier to express a desire for certain goods or situations than the reason, the motive behind that choice.

The Coach Leader encourages people to discover and acknowledge the value behind their every need.

The following observation is interesting: **When the need is met, it is no longer a motive**. This means that in order to activate a person, something else is needed.

Values, on the other hand, persist and are always a motive. So, it is obvious that in order to motivate people over the long term, you need to know the value that represents them and triggers their desire.

I analyse the history of motivation in detail in my book, *The Art of Peace in the Workplace*. I refer to all the motivation theories as they have evolved from the industrial revolution and the first occupational psychologists to date. It's very interesting to know their evolution.

Coach Leaders who know the values of their team members can better understand and activate them. Moreover, they can gain their commitment toward a common higher purpose that they co-create considering their values.

Values are a constant point of reference that empower you. They help you set healthy boundaries, and healthy boundaries give you strength. When you share that strength with other people, you form deeper and more meaningful connections.

People who express their values within a common, higher purpose are committed to it and to all the separate goals—actions needed to achieve that purpose.

6.2.3. Prerequisite: self-knowledge

To uncover the values of their team and increase their engagement with the common goal, Coach Leaders first need to discover their personal values, their own **WHY**.

People's motivation originates from their personal values, which give them a sense of what is really important to them.

Everything that is authentic and original, like the values of every human being, is also timeless. One question I usually get from my clients is whether these values change over time. I believe that some authentic values that are important and truly representative remain unaltered.

At the beginning of each coaching relationship, I support my clients to discover their most important values through a deep and liberating process. I realised that their most representative values do not change over time.

What happens is that priorities change, or more values are added. Identifying our values is a never-ending process, always evolving, so that we can determine, whenever necessary, our priorities and make the right decisions.

> The journey of self-knowledge has many intermediate stops but only one destination: self-knowledge and eudaimonia.

Values are a compass that helps people reach their potential, grow, and be happy.

I close this subsection with a beautiful excerpt from *On Stage Without Rehearsal*, written by Athens University of Economics and Business professor Dimitris Bourantas:

"Values are the cohesive web, the reference axis that brings you back to what is right and wrong behaviour. They are the rules that tell you what the limits are, what you can reach with your energies, your ambitions, your dreams."

6.3. Existential orientation

Leadership through values urges toward an existential orientation. Coach Leaders discover people's values—thus, their inner desires, their motivations—and then develop them toward a meaningful life. They give people the opportunity and necessary space to discover and express their values.

People now have an important reason (the **WHY**) to follow, to commit to, and to fight for a common vision that includes, at some point, their own values.

Coach Leaders are activated and activate others because:

1. They uncover their own values.
2. They uncover the values of their team members.

3. They create together with their team a common vision that includes these values.

Vision and values are the best orientation for each person separately and for a team as a whole. This orientation is called "existential" because it stems from life values and includes a higher meaning. Coaching has a lot in common with the **humanitarian existential psychotherapy** of Irvin Yalom and Rollo May without, in any way, addressing patients.

> The Coach Leader is the leader that inspires and supports people toward an existential orientation with the purpose of holistic development and eudaimonia.

I wish to close this section with the disarming words of Irvin Yalom from his book *Creatures of a Day*:

"Once again, I felt very humble in the face of the immense complexity of the human mind and at the same time, I despaired of the vagueness that characterises Psychiatry's attempts to simplify, codify and compile technical manuals for the pre-planned treatment of patients. In my office I had two patients who travelled to the ocean of wisdom of a rare human and each of them was able to draw something different that helped them in a way that neither I nor anyone else would have predicted."

From this moving passage, I would suggest that you keep the **humility** of the great professor and psychotherapist Irvin Yalom, who recognises his limits and bows before the superiority and uniqueness of human thought and behaviour.

Coach Leaders should also be characterised by a humble knowledge of their limits.

> **Summarising**
>
> There are no behavioural manuals to teach you with 100% accuracy what is appropriate to do as a leader in each case.
>
> I suggest you look at the people of your team as a white sheet of paper, and the pencil to write on it belonging only to themselves.
>
> Your duty is to help them remain strong and open so that they can write their own script and be the **protagonists of their own lives**.

POINTS TO REMEMBER FROM STEP 6

- The Coach Leader's key tool is the discovery of their personal values and then the values of their team.
- Values are the evolution of classical virtues.
- If I want change, I should first practice it myself and then motivate and support my team to achieve it.
- Coaching leadership is not another leadership model but a way of life that is practiced daily in every condition.

PHILOSOPHICAL LEADERSHIP

YOUR TURN

Immediate action I will take:

Are there any obstacles? If so, what are they?

How will I overcome each obstacle?

STEP 7

PHILOSOPHERSHIP™: THE PHILOSOPHICAL MODEL OF LEADERSHIP

"Self-awareness and the pursuit of a higher purpose inspire and strengthen inner leadership and form the basis of the model."

— BARBARA ASIMAKOPOULOU

PURPOSE

The purpose of the seventh step is to equip Coach Leaders with a practical strategic and decision-making model that suits their personality and higher purpose, a model that will support coachees to achieve their goals and unlock their full potential.

Every person—even more so, a leader—before passing from thought to action, inquires, discovers, plans, and utilises the resources (means) at their disposal.

Coach Leaders do the same, equipped with the right strategic and decision-making models. What distinguishes the models we use in coaching from any other model is their starting point, **self-knowledge**.

When there is complexity, it is better to understand reality before taking the necessary action. We should clarify the current situation and identify the bigger picture—that is, the essence that gives meaning and motive to every feeling and action. Strategic models reduce complexity and confusion by making it easier for us to focus on the most important elements.

In the sections that follow, I present to you the **Philosophership™** model, the **philosophical model of leadership**—strategy and action based on classical philosophy—which I have created and have been practicing successfully.

7.1. The main idea behind the model

The core idea behind the model is a timeless and universal philosophical observation, summarised in the following sentence:

Each person must look to themselves to discover the meaning of their life.

And why is this?

Because when a person discovers the fundamental purpose of their existence, regardless of when they make this discovery, it marks the beginning of a better life.

According to **Aristotle** and **Maslow**, when this destination is reached, they gain self-actualisation. According to Socrates, they gain the "good life": happiness through a virtuous life.

The search for life's meaning is a fundamental existential and philosophical principle.

"I exist," according to **Sartre**, means I create the meaning of my life. I create a place I rightfully belong to, and I am happy in it.

Some people discover their meaning in social contribution or creative expression.

According to **Richard Barrett**, maturity leads people to transcend individual ambitions and enter the last step in his hierarchy of human needs: the period of social responsibility and contribution. The discovery of this greater purpose and its daily pursuit fills people with liberation, inner satisfaction, and joy.

As we mature, our existential purpose becomes clearer and the journey more enjoyable. Wisdom and awareness are some of the rewards of getting older.

> Wisdom is the virtue we acquire with growing experience and knowledge of ourselves and our environment.
>
> This virtue brings us closer to inner leadership and inner emancipation.

7.2. Philosophy for social change

This model can be used in the pursuit of a higher purpose that transcends individual satisfaction, especially when society is in urgent need of changes that will ensure the viability of the human race.

Modern philosophers, such as **Michael Sandel**, **Thomas Pogge**, **Martha Nussbaum**, **Will Kymlicka**, **Cornelius Castoriadis**, and **Stelios Ramfos**, argue that philosophy needs to be involved in the deep and difficult questions of **how** and **why** we should live together as social beings.

They suggest that **philosophy has the potential to change the way we live as individuals and prompt a wider social change.**

Plato's Republic, ruled by philosophers, is a strong example of how philosophy can bring about social change.

7.3. Human participation

I believe that we do not need to have Aristotle's or Sartre's unparalleled depth and breadth of thought to discover the meaning of our lives and achieve our goals. Similarly, it is not necessary to be Alexander the Great to effectively lead a team, such as a social, political, or business team, or even our families.

We should take due note of the knowledge these magnificent thinkers have offered us in order to reflect and better plan our future and live the life we deserve.

With the **Philosophership™** model, we bring the best of the human intellect into our daily practice **so that we can live a meaningful life**. The Philosophership™ model answers the question of **Mihaly Csikszentmihalyi**: *What makes a life worth living?*

7.4. Philosophical coaching

The purpose of every coach and Coach Leader, as I propose with this book, is to support every individual to **integrate philosophy into their daily lives**. According to the famous dictum uttered by Socrates at his trial:

PHILOSOPHICAL LEADERSHIP

"The unexamined life is not worth living."

— SOCRATES, *PLATO, APOLOGY*, 38A

A life that is not philosophically and existentially examined is not worth living.

This famous statement is found in Plato's dialogue "Apology," which recounts Socrates' defense during his trial in Athens.

In the "Apology," Socrates is addressing the jury and defending his philosophical activities. He argues that his commitment to examining his own life and the lives of others is essential to a meaningful existence. (Plato, Apology, 38a)

This quote has become one of the most well-known and enduring philosophical statements associated with Socrates and his emphasis on self-reflection, the pursuit of knowledge, and the value of examining one's own life in the quest for wisdom and understanding.

Coaching helps people discover their ideal purpose—a higher, meaningful purpose that attracts them so much that they can overcome any obstacle in the pursuit of their goals and true happiness.

Jaqueline de Romilly, (1913–2010) an esteemed Franco-Greek scholar and specialist on Ancient Greek theatre, admired the Ancient Greek way of life because it incorporated joy and sorrow as two sides of the same coin.

Coaches support coachees to discover a higher personal purpose that helps them live harmoniously with joy and sorrow—that is, with the opportunities and challenges of life.

A purpose that allows them to not be discouraged by difficulties and continue their lives, like the Ancient Greeks, who welcomed both joy and sorrow and faced with miraculous acceptance any tragedy the gods brought upon them.

The Philosophership™ model borrows from philosophy to enhance the process of self-discovery, to activate and transform the coachee.

Philosophy and the meaning of life

Since ancient times, all philosophers have sought the meaning of life. They have examined the origin and cause of human existence, the reason for living—what should we ask of life and how should we relate to others?

I wonder why they went to so much trouble. Why have so many eminent philosophers spent their lives on these questions?

This question might seem useless or insignificant to some, but it is a fact that philosophers have devoted millions of hours to analysing, reflecting upon, and communicating their ideas on these profound issues.

Allow me to answer the above questions, according to my own perception and interpretation.

The word "philosopher" means someone who *loves* wisdom—that is, knowledge.

According to Professor Babiniotis' *Dictionary of Synonyms and Antonyms*, philosophy is a combination of two Greek words, "philein" and "sophia," meaning *lover of wisdom*. It is synonymous with worldview, way of thinking, perception, wisdom, knowledge, and good judgment. I conclude that the philosopher's motive is curiosity for any new or pre-existing knowledge and the search for truth.

At the same time, perhaps the greatest motivation behind this search is the **human drive** to find answers to the fundamental questions of life and death.

Let us summarise:
Philosophers seek the meaning of life; this is their job, their responsibility.

Our job is to live the life we deserve, a life of meaning!

How?

I suggest we use the legacy bequeathed to us by so many amazing philosophers. They taught us how to live through their unique and wonderful work, reflecting their intellect and wisdom.

We have 2500 years of philosophical thinking at our disposal!

Philosophy shows us **how** to live every day and **why**, the meaning (value–motivation) behind our actions. Specifically, philosophy suggests the appropriate behaviour (how) towards an ideal purpose that is different for each person (what and why).

With the help of a coach, you will choose the path (how) and the orientation (what and why) that corresponds to your personal values and your unique personality.

I present in detail the model that encapsulates all of the above in 7.5. Philosphership™: The Model.

7.5. PHILOSOPHERSHIP™: THE MODEL

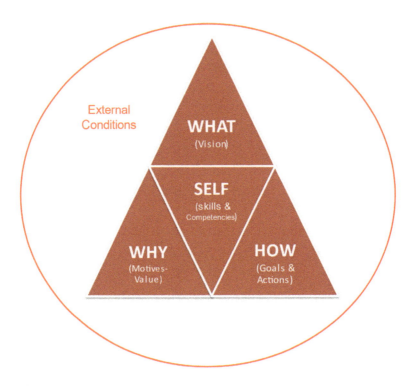

Figure 7.5. shows the Philosophical Leadership Model - Philosophership™.

You can see in Figure 7.5., the model has self-knowledge (SELF) at the core and the triptych, which includes the:

- WHAT
- WHY
- HOW.

SELF

As in all coaching models, the background for every planning and decision-making process is self-knowledge. Specifically, you need to know and, if not, discover your strengths, weaknesses, abilities, skills, and talents.

The Ancient Greek quotation "know thyself," inscribed on Apollo's temple at Delphi, affirms self-knowledge as an experience that requires great effort. According to Professor Babiniotis, ethical philosophy ultimately aims at the achievement of self-knowledge.

Therefore, self-knowledge is at the core of my philosophical model. In my opinion, it is the beginning and end of every action, every new knowledge or experience. It is a chapter of our life that is constantly being enriched.

Self-awareness has a psychological content and refers to the consciousness of our existence as opposed to the existence of others. Another related word is "self-consciousness." Coaching, introspection, self-observation, and self-reflection are all techniques that lead to the acquisition of self-knowledge.

WHY

The "why" is your motivation: the reason behind your action, the fuel that provides the energy you need to pursue the path of your choice.

It is important to diagnose your motivation and why you desire that particular life orientation. Every person's motivation stems from their personal values. The inner motives, aspirations, and priorities for the key areas of your life. Deep and authentic desires, such as creativity, adventure, risk-taking, freedom, enjoyment, spirituality, companionship, achievement, creativity, success, and contribution.

It is also necessary to separate the values from the needs because they are often confused. There is always a true value behind every need, as described in the *previews* step.

Example: Someone wants to buy a fast sports car. Transportation is a need. The value behind this need may be adventure, risk, or ostentation, depending on the person's profile.

An additional difference between values and needs is that needs, when met, cease to be a motivator, while values remain. In the example above, the owner of the fast sports car meets their need for that car when they buy it, and it ceases to be an incentive. But the value of adventure, risk, or ostentation remains.

Every value leads to actions and behaviours that bring satisfaction. Some people know what their values are, while others do not.

Most people, however, do not suspect that behind every action or repressed desire there is a hidden value, a part of their true self.

Values are the solid part of yourself, your point of reference, your beacon, your guiding light, during every change or situation. They help you make decisions, clarify goals, and set or redefine your destination every time it is needed.

Knowing your personal values and sharing them with others helps you connect, keeps you authentic and motivated, and guides you toward the appropriate behaviour. Values determine what is important; therefore, they define your priorities.

Thus, when you do not have clear values, you do not have clear priorities.

Only by knowing yourself and your true desires can you plan your destination where you will be happy.

To summarise, values are the fuel to set priorities and make the right decisions to move your life in the right direction.

I recommend you first discover them *and then* visualise your ideal destination.

WHAT

What is your ideal destination? What is your "Ithaca"? Do you know exactly where you want to go, what you want to achieve, what you want to enjoy in life? What are the important things in your life that you should not neglect? Do you have a personal vision?

Personal vision activates you and helps you navigate in the face of adversity. Your vision inspires you, makes you dedicate yourself to the right goals and implement the right strategies and actions to achieve them.

Having a clear and attractive destination (the "what") lights up the path and clears your mind of confusion so you can safely start your journey. The more attractive the destination is, the more likely you are to overcome the obstacles that you encounter.

Values (the why) speak to your *heart*.

Vision (the what) speaks to your *mind*. It is an attractive place, and when you mentally or practically take yourself there, you feel absolute satisfaction.

> **IMPORTANT**
>
> According to this model, your life serves a higher purpose—a higher purpose that includes your legacy and a positive influence on a particular group or your immediate environment. The more people you influence, the greater your responsibility to influence for a good cause for all.

HOW

Once you know your values (why) and your desired destination (what), you are ready to define your strategy, how you will reach it.

Strategy includes the goals and actions you will undertake to follow your life orientation honouring your values. I would also add the personal relationships you will nurture and the means you will use, your resources.

Goals are important desired results that bring you, step by step, closer to your vision. They are quantitative or qualitative. The number of goals that we can practically manage, based on my knowhow and experience, is four to five. These goals derive from your personal vision and express your values.

> My suggestion is to achieve the life you deserve through planning and not by chance, even if the path to happiness requires a lot of changes to the plan!

Example: Two of my most important values are creativity and human interaction. My vision is that by being a great coach, author, speaker, and an inspirational leader in my profession, I can positively influence as many people as possible.

One of the 4–5 goals I have set in order to achieve my vision is to ensure that my knowledge and skills are up-to-date and of exceptional quality.

Goals are the desired results that activate you in the right direction and measure your performance. An added advantage of goal setting is that it focuses your attention on important issues and encourages better distribution of your resources (mind, energy, money, time, people).

Then, you plan the necessary actions to achieve each goal.

These actions are the steps that lead you to your vision and help you enjoy the life you have while you create the life of your dreams.

According to the above example, to achieve my own goal of high-quality knowledge and skills, one action I need to take is to receive ongoing and systematic training or support by the best professionals and organisations.

"Do you want to have experiences that fit in a thimble or in a barrel?" as **Anthony Robbins** (popular life coach) characteristically says.

People can spend an eternity waiting for the right moment and preparing for something they desire without ever taking any action to achieve it.

For example, one of my clients received a very good coaching training and the necessary knowledge, technique, and tools. However, she constantly postponed testing it in the market on the pretext that she was not ready and needed more training. Instead of also investing in marketing and sales, she was only investing in new coaching skills. But this choice was not helping her attract customers.

Caution: Continuous preparation and procrastination can be a sign of internal barriers, such as prejudices or restricting beliefs. However, the right timing of any action is crucial.

Procrastination is common in many people, and it is one of the biggest internal barriers to happiness.

Conclusion: **planning is good, but action is even better!**

It is also vital to systematically evaluate the progress of your goals. Follow-up and monitoring allow for change, offer satisfaction, boost your self-esteem and confidence, and, of course, bring you closer to the fulfilment of your desires.

External conditions

You may have noticed that, in the representation of the model in Figure 7.5., the external conditions are placed outside the triangle. We will now consider these conditions that exist outside the triangle of personal life planning.

Are the conditions of your environment favourable or restrictive?

Whatever the external conditions, you need to find a way to use them to your advantage. You need to make the necessary adjustments and continue your journey toward your destination. Do a macroscopic study of the strengths, weaknesses, opportunities, and threats of the environment (SWOT analysis). Consider all the economic, political, social, technological, or other fields that affect your vision.

The external environment can be either favourable or disadvantageous. I suggest you (a) ignore what you cannot influence and (b) find a way to overcome what stands in your way or use it to your advantage.

Using an obstacle to your advantage or discovering the positive in the negative is a method of **re-framing** and a sign of lateral thinking and resourcefulness.

Appropriate use of the model and the coach's contribution

At all stages of the model, coaches support coachees to discover their personal values, to envision and describe their higher purpose, to find their life meaning, to plan their strategy, and to overcome internal and external obstacles. Finally, they enable them to enjoy the whole journey. Coaches inspire their coachees to pursue a meaningful life and not ignore or leave it to chance.

Coaches guide their coachees to pursue a higher attractive purpose beyond restricting personal ambitions, not fearing what they might lose but full of faith for what they will gain.

POINTS TO REMEMBER FROM STEP 7

- The Philosophership™ leadership model. Correct use of it will maximise your potential.
- Self-knowledge is the necessary foundation of every decision-making process.
- The existential orientation and the search for a meaningful life and a higher purpose will help leaders and coaches to be powerful and impactful.
- Visualisation motivates and inspires.
- Planning, commitment, and consistent actions make the dream a reality.
- Among the basic principles of human behaviour, the search for a higher purpose that inspires and justifies human choices and actions occupies a key position.
- Coaches support people in the search for but also the achievement of this great goal.

*"Vision without action is just a dream,
action without vision just passes the time.
Vision with action can change the world!"*

— JOEL A. BARKER, AMERICAN AUTHOR,
SPEAKER, AND FUTURIST

PHILOSOPHICAL LEADERSHIP

YOUR TURN

Immediate action I will take:

Are there any obstacles? If so, what are they?

How will I overcome each obstacle?

STEP 8

FIRST-TIME LEADER

"From individual performance and omnipotence to team performance and crew services."

— BARBARA ASIMAKOPOULOU

PURPOSE

The eighth step aims to get you acquainted with the new conditions and challenges that arise when taking on the role of the leader, to help you understand the skills required by the new role, and finally, to equip you with the right strategies to excel.

8.1. The new conditions and challenges

Undoubtedly, one of the most critical moments is when a leader takes on the role for the first time. But this is also the case for experienced leaders who take on a new team in a new organisation.

During the adjustment period, the new leader needs to consider many factors:

- the relationships with the team and the people who influence it (managers, partners, suppliers, customers, etc.)
- the culture
- the strategic location
- the industry
- the knowledge and skills that are likely required.

Surveys show a high failure rate during this transition period. Moreover, the higher the position of the new leader, the higher the cost to the company in the event of failure. Successful adaptation to the new role is very important for all involved.

During this crucial adaptation period, coaching is the best help; it acts as a catalyst throughout the process and quickly brings the highest added value to the organisation.

8.2. The new role

The new leader who takes on the role is overwhelmed by emotions. There are positive feelings of joy and satisfaction but also negative ones, such as anxiety and fear of failure. Their immediate environment (family, friends, colleagues) can easily perceive the change and usually act as magnifiers for the above positive or negative emotions.

The new leader's mind is full of ideas and creative thoughts to meet the new challenges. An enjoyable and promising introduction to this new era.

But are the leaders prepared enough to ensure success?

Of course—as long as they realise that the new era is different from the previous one. They reached their new position of leadership by relying on their personal efforts, skills, and knowledge. Their individual performance served the interests of the organisation and helped them achieve their goals.

But the role of the leader, manager, or team coordinator is quite different from any previous individual role.

The challenges

People who lead a team have special qualifications and responsibilities that one may be unaware of.

Managers are tasked with effectively managing human resources, time, energy, and other material resources, such as money, supplies, and infrastructure. Their role is to **make excellent use of all resources** and bring the desired results in keeping with the mission and philosophy of the organisation.

> The purpose of the new leader is to bring results, not only through individual work and performance but mainly through the work and performance of their team.

8.3. New way of working

To successfully achieve their new mission, new leaders need new skills and a new way of thinking and working.

The **new way of working** requires a shift in mindset and, in particular, a **change of focus**. The new leader needs to move quickly from individual focus to team focus and effective management.

The skills required have more to do with human resource management, motivation, communication, and teamwork.

More walking than talking

During the first weeks of their term, before they can begin designing their strategy, new leaders have to gain the trust of their team members and of all those in the parallel or vertical hierarchy. Establishing this as a priority will allow them to gain the **acceptance and credibility that are necessary to start their great work**.

People's trust is not a given; people's trust is gained. New leaders should prioritise getting to know their people, building good communication, and cultivating interaction and co-creation. The above components form the basis for effective leadership.

Figure 8.3. The process of growth

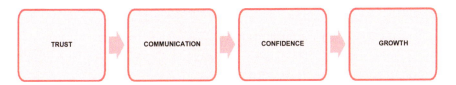

Figure 8.3. shows the process of growth and its foundations, that is TRUST.

New leaders are required to know well:

- the responsibilities, the people, and the work performed in their department
- the culture, the particularities, and the conditions of the department
- the relations with other departments, and especially those with which they cooperate directly
- the key people.

Questionnaire research and SWOT analysis will help them discover the new environment quickly and efficiently.

The sooner they get the information they need, the sooner they will feel secure and confident.

I cannot stress it enough that the biggest effort has to do with **getting to know the people**!

> The new leader needs to shift from the omnipotence of the superhero, which begins and ends with individual battle, to the superpower of the crew.

The **360°** feedback test for self-awareness (gathering information from coworkers, friends, superiors, subordinates, customers, etc.) and discovering their strengths and areas of improvement will help them see what they need to change or strengthen.

Moreover, working with a coach is strongly recommended.

8.4. Common mistakes

Individual success does not guarantee team success
The selection of a new manager is often based on the wrong criteria—mainly on the good results the candidate has achieved in previous positions where they worked individually, without considering the necessary leadership skills to work with a team.

> Keep the suitcase from the previous trip but prepare a new one for the new trip!

Sticking to the same routine

A common mistake new managers make to overcome their fear of the unknown created by the new position is to occupy themselves with what they did before they became manager. They stay in the comfort zone of their previous habits and continue to do what they know well.

This behaviour leads to the wrong path; they lose time, self-esteem, and credibility, and they do not bring the expected results.

Arrogance

Experienced managers should repress the feeling of omnipotence fuelled by their knowledge and experience. Strong self-confidence ends up being an obstacle when it impedes feedback from the team.

It would be beneficial for the new leader to accept that, at least at the beginning, other team members will know things that they may not know. They need to ask for feedback and learn from them.

Not utilising the human resources of the team

Sometimes, new managers end up taking care of everything because, as they claim, there is not enough time to train people and delegate responsibilities.

This practice, in the long run, creates irresponsible and incompetent partners.

Getting lost in urgent and daily tasks

New managers are often sidetracked by the daily routine instead of planning and organising the work. In these cases, the team's performance, as well as their own, will be randomly good and, most of the time, defective.

Not seeing the forest for the trees

They do not evaluate the priorities of the department/team according to the central vision but address them randomly and impulsively according to the priorities of others (e.g., suppliers, other departments, etc.).

Each team is a small business where managers need to maintain the vision and inspire accordingly, as well as delegate responsibilities, evaluate, and support.

8.5. From personal effectiveness to teamwork

Leaders, when they are called to lead a team for the first time, need to change their mentality and professional behaviour.

It is crucial to go beyond the familiar and safe habit of previous knowledge and start exercising their managerial skills immediately.

The new individual skills

The individual skills required by the new position are different from those required by their previous successful career as a team member.

Skills such as:

- the art of active listening
- composing instead of analysing

- seeking the opinion of others
- allowing people to find the solution themselves
- speaking last
- delegating
- coordinating
- inspiring and rewarding
- co-creating
- being a Coach Leader!

People who work alone can implement things automatically, without having to ask for the opinion of others. As a leader, you need to develop a communication code that is recognised, understood, and accepted by all team members.

Leaders influence the people around them, even without speaking, and that is a big responsibility.

Internal motivation

Effective leadership of a team depends on the internal motivation of the leader, the deep reason that makes them consciously strive and plan for success.

The new leader gains significant support by utilising other people's knowledge and experience. A leadership education, along with a mentor or/and a coach, could be of great value.

> It should not be taken for granted that a successful employee has the skills to perform equally well in a new position that requires them to lead a team.

8.6. Strategies to lead a team in the beginning

In this subsection, I present the best strategies for taking up a new leadership role successfully.

When there is already leadership experience

Leaders who have already exercised their managerial skills need to continue with the same enthusiasm and care.

As people are unique, the management of a new team is likely to require adjustments or changes.

Knowledge means power.

The knowledge that you lack, others have it.

Do not be afraid to admit it and get it as soon as possible.

The excellent reputation you have gained from your previous position gives you the key to opening the knowledge portal of your new one. The sooner you do it, the sooner you gain trust, credibility, and self-confidence—qualities necessary to engage others in action.

Steps to win your team as a first-time leader

Being a team leader is challenging, but it allows you to apply your ideas and write your chapter in the bestseller of the organisation you work for.

Successful adaptation strategies:

- focus on success through the team, not just yourself
- quickly acquire the knowledge you need to feel safe and confident
- forge the right alliances
- work with a coach.

Practice your managerial skills:

- get people engaged in your vision. Co-create the shared vision of the team
- design a systematic and accessible communication channel
- gain the trust of your people
- co-create the strategy
- coordinate and motivate your team toward a higher goal that is gratifying for everyone
- empower—develop your people
- reward—celebrate with your team
- systematically monitor, evaluate, and review actions
- enrol in a coaching leadership program.

Learn to use tools:

- business plan
- project planning
- time and energy management
- meditation—mindfulness
- personal branding
- NLP (neuro-linguistic programming)

- effective discussions
- 360° evaluation tests
- coaching tools.

Prepare for the next promotion:

- develop personal development strategies
- invest in yourself
- make your successes known
- work with a coach
- establish balance—mental, physical, and emotional.

8.7. The role of coaching for the new leader

The significant support of the coach. Having the support of a coach from the beginning is crucial because they help you:

- adapt quickly to the new environment and start performing
- present your best self
- diagnose your team's conditions, environment, opportunities, and challenges
- develop your personal signature
- create a shared vision with your team
- make the most of your people
- motivate them
- delegate responsibilities
- overcome internal and external obstacles
- maintain your balance
- remain satisfied and happy throughout the process

- solve problems and support others to solve them
- increase your self-confidence
- immerse yourself in the art of communication
- prepare for your next promotion.

10 rules for effective adaptation to the new role

1. Focus on success through the team, not just yourself.
2. Quickly acquire the knowledge you need to feel confident.
3. Forge the right alliances.
4. Prepare your strategy.
5. Practice your managerial skills.
6. Gain trust.
7. Co-create a common inspirational vision.
8. Design the action plan with your team.
9. Empower, motivate, and reward your team.
10. Work with a coach.

Coach the leader

The coach's presence is crucial in achieving not only the goals but also personal satisfaction and growth.

The Coach Leader is tasked with developing the people in their team, and the coach is called to develop the leader.

The new professional challenge requires different skills than the previous role. It has more to do with human resource management, communication, delegating responsibilities, coaching, and creating a **new way of working**.

> There is a shift of focus from personal growth to team development and effective management.

Coaching facilitates the desired change, enhances growth, and creates a Coach Leader who will undertake the demanding work of human development and act as a role model and moral compass toward a sustainable and prosperous society.

POINTS TO REMEMBER FROM STEP 8

- The new leader undertakes a project full of challenges but, simultaneously, they can leave their mark.
- The role of the new leader is to bring results, not only through their personal work but through other people.
- The new leader is also responsible for other resources, such as time, money, and infrastructure.
- The skills required are human resource management, motivation, communication, teamwork, and coaching.
- The presence of a coach during this process is a catalyst for the development of the new leader and their team.
- The new leader acts as a role model and a moral compass.

YOUR TURN

Immediate action I will take:

Are there any obstacles? If so, what are they?

How will I overcome each obstacle?

AFTERWORD

The Coach Leader uses coaching leadership, the only model of everyday leadership that brings out the best traits of human mind and soul.

Coaching leadership is a way of life, not just another leadership model.

You have the choice to set the example for a sustainable and human-centred society by manifesting emotions such as love, respect, and appreciation for yourself and your beloved human beings, and ideal behavioural patterns such as wisdom, compassion, gratitude, and forgiveness.

Jesus Christ is an exemplary leader and vast object of study.

Therefore, I would like to close this book with an excerpt from "Sermon on the Mount," which is considered one of the most poetic and timeless texts to have greatly influenced Western philosophy.

"You are the light of the world. A city set on a hill cannot be hidden. Nor do people light a lamp and put it under a basket, but on a stand, and it gives light to all in the house. In the same way, let your light shine before others, so that they may see your good works and give glory to your Father who is in heaven."

May you become the light of the world, with humility and gratitude for the opportunity you have. Do not ignore it.

In *The Nicomachean Ethics*, Aristotle states that we acquire virtues by practicing them, just as we do in the arts—the things we have to learn, we learn by doing.

Beautiful results come into our lives through consistent practice of the new behaviour that finally becomes a beneficial habit.

Whether you are an active or potential leader, your first achievement is your own life.

Take control, dream, plan routes, love yourself, break free from suffocating conventions, gain the coveted inner emancipation, and finally be a catalyst for positive change, creating authentic, responsible, and happy people.

My sincere thanks,
Barbara Asimakopoulou

RECOMMENDED BIBLIOGRAPHY

In English

Alkistis Agio, 2020, *From Fear to Freedom*, independently published.

Amy Brann, 2017, *Neuroscience for Coaches*, Kogan Page.

Brené Brown, 2021, *Atlas of the Heart*, Random House.

Chris Gill, 2013, *Marcus Aurelius, Meditation Book 1–6*, Oxford University Press.

Daniel Goleman, 2013, *Focus: The Hidden Driver of Excellence*, Bloomsbury Publishing.

Daniel Kahneman, 2012, *Thinking Fast and Slow*, Penguin.

Dave Drake, 2017, *Narrative Coaching: The Definitive Guide to Bringing New Stories to Life*, CNC Press.

Dean Burnett, 2018, *The Happy Brain*, Guardian Faber Publishing.

Dimitris Bourantas, Vasia Agapitou, 2016, *Leadership Meta-Competencies: Discovering Hidden Virtues*, Routledge.

Donald Robertson, 2013, *Stoicism and the Art of Happiness*, Teach Yourself.

Donald Robertson, 2019, *How to Think Like a Roman Emperor: The Stoic Philosophy of Marcus Aurelius*, Macmillan Audio.

Hetty Einzig, 2017, *The Future of Coaching*, Routledge.

Howard Gardner, 1983, *Frames of Mind: The Theory of Multiple Intelligences*, Basic Books.

Irvin Yalom, 2008, *Staring at the Sun*, Jossey-Bass.

Irvin Yalom, 1999, *Momma and the Meaning of Life*, Basic Books.

Jenny Rogers, 2008, *Coaching Skills: A Handbook*, Open University Press/McGraw-Hill.

Jenny Rogers, Arti Maini, 2016, *Coaching for Health*, Open University Press/McGraw-Hill.

John C. Maxwell, 1993, *Develop the Leader Within You*, Thomas Nelson.

John C. Maxwell, 2014, *JumpStart your Leadership*, Center Street.

John Whitmore, 2009, *Coaching for Performance*, Nicholas Brealey Publishing.

Jonathan Passmore & Tracy Sinclaire, 2020, *Becoming a Coach: The Essential ICF Guide*, Springer.

Judith E. Glaser, 2016, *Conversational Intelligence: How Great Leaders Build Trust and Get Extraordinary Results*, Routledge.

Jules Evans, 2013, *Philosophy for Life and Other Dangerous Situations*, Random House.

Julie Starr, 2021, *The Coaching Manual*, Pearson.

Julio Olalla, 2004, *From Knowledge to Wisdom: Essays on the Crisis in the Contemporary Learning*, Newfield Network, Inc.

Ken Wilber, 1996, *A Brief History of Everything*, Shambhala.

Kets De Vries, 2014, *Mindfulness Leadership Coaching*, Palgrave Macmillan.

Marsall Goldsmith, Mark Reiter, 2015, *Triggers*, Crown Business.

Marsall Goldsmith, Sally Helgesen, 2018, *How Women Rise*, Hachette Books.

Marshall Goldsmith, 2022, *The Earned Life*, Currency Editions.

Marshall Goldsmith, A. Weiss, 2017, *Lifestorming: Creating Meaning and Achievement in Your Career and Life*, Wiley.

Marshall Goldsmith, M. Reiter, 2007, *What Got You Here Won't Get You There*, Random House.

- Martin Seligman, 2011, *Flourish: A Visionary New Understanding of Happiness and Well-being*, Free Press.

Martin Seligman, 2014, *Authentic Happiness: Using the New Positive Psychology to Realize Your Potential for Lasting Fulfillment*, Atria Books.

Mihaly Csikszentmihalyi, 2014, *Flow and the Foundations of Positive Psychology: The Collected Works of Mihaly Csikszentmihalyi*, Springer.

Mikael Krogerus, Roman Tschäppeler, 2012, *The Decision Book*, W. W. Norton & Company.

Monica Hanaway, 2019, *The Existential Leader*, Routledge.

Nathan Jamail, 2014, *The Leadership Playbook*, Gotham Books.

Peter Hawkins, 2017, *Leadership Team Coaching*, Kogan Page.

Ryan Holiday, 2019, *Stillness is the Key*, Penguin.

Richard Barrett, 2010, *The New Leadership Paradigm*, Barrett Editions.

Richard Barrett, 2014, *Evolutionary Coaching: A Values-Based Approach to Unleashing Human Potential*, Barrett Editions.

Richard Barrett, 2017, *The Values-Driven Organization: Cultural Health and Employee Well-Being as a Pathway to Sustainable Performance*, Barrett Editions.

Roger Sheare, 2009, *Ethicability*, Roger Steare Consulting Limited.

Sally Helgesen, 2023, *Rising Together: How We Can Bridge Divides and Create a More Inclusive Workplace*, Hachette Book Group.

Simon Sinek, 2014, *Leaders Eat Last*, Portfolio Penguin.

Sylviane Cannio, Viviane Lauren, 2011, *Coaching Excellence: Best Practices in Business Coaching*, LID Publishing.

Thomas G. Crane, 2002, *The Heart of Coaching*, FTA Press.

Thomas Leonard, 2007, *28 Laws of Attraction*, Scribner.

Tim LeBon, 2014, *Achieve Your Potential with Positive Psychology*, Hodder & Stoughton.

Timothy Gallwey, 2008, *The Inner Game of Tennis*, Random House.

Tünde Erdös, 2021, *Coaching Presence, Understand the Power of Non-Verbal Relationship*, Applied Sciences Publishing.

Tünde Erdös, Angelis Inglesias, 2020, *The Coaching Science-Practitioner Handbook*, Applied Sciences Publishing.

Yannick Jacobs, 2019, *Existential Coaching*, Routledge.

In Greek

Anna Karamanou, 2022, *The Peaceful Protesting of Female Sapiens*, Armos.

Antony Robbins, 2016, *Unlimited Power: Push Your Limits*, Dioptra.

Aristotle, 2004, *On Drunkenness, On Virtues and Vices, About the World*, Zitros.

Aristotle, 2006, *Nicomachean Ethics*, Zitros.

Barbara Asimakopoulou, 2008, *The Art of Peace in the Workplace*, Kritiki Publishing.

Barbara Asimakopoulou, 2021, *Inner Emancipation*, HRE Publishing.

Barbara Asimakopoulou, 2022, *Self Reflections: The Coach's Journal*, HRE Publishing.

Charles Pepin, 2011, *Philosophers on the Sofa: Freud Meets Plato, Kant and Sartre*, Contemporary Horizons.

Daniel Goleman, Richard Boyatzis, Annie Mckee, 2014, *The New Leader*, Pedio.

Daniel Goleman, 1998, *Working with Emotional Intelligence*, Greek Letters Edition.

Dimitris Bouradas, 2005, *Leadership*, Kritiki.

Dimitris Bouradas, 2015, *The Great Philosophers and Personal Management*, Patakis.

Dimitris Bourantas, 2010, *On Stage Without Rehearsal*, Patakis.

Epikouros, 2009, *The Moral Treatment of the Soul*, Zitros.

George Chatzivasilas, 2019, *The Road to Self-Knowledge*, Ydroplano.

Haridimos Tsoukas, 2004, *If Aristotle was CEO*, Kastaniotis Editions.

Irvin Yalom, 2015, *Creatures of a Day*, Agra.

James O'Toole, 2006, *Creating the Good Life: Applying Aristotle's Wisdom to Find Meaning and Happiness*, Enalios.

Jim Collins, 2005, *Good to Great*, Klitharithmos.
Jostein Gaarder, 1994, *Sophie's World: A Novel on the History of Philosophy*, Livanis.
Leonidas Georgiadis, 2017, *Lessons of Philosophy*, Georgiadis Publishing.
Leonidas Georgiadis, 2021, *Well Being Series: The Management of Negative Emotions According to the Stoics*, Psichogios.
Leonidas Georgiadis, 2023, *Well Being Series: The Management of Positive Emotions According to the Stoics*, Psichogios.
Lou Marinov, 1999, *Plato, Not Prozac: The Application of Philosophy to Everyday Problems*, Levanis.
Louis-Andre Dorion, 2007, *Socrates*, Lamprakis.
Maria Antoniadou, 2022, *Applying the Humanities and Core Coaching Principles to the Health Sciences*, Tsotras Publishing.
Mihaly Csikszentmihalyi, 2009, *Flow: The Psychology of Optimal Experience*, Kastaniotis Publications.
Mimis Androulakis, 2015, *Black Box*, Patakis Publications.
Nigel Warburton, 2011, *A Short History of Philosophy*, Pataki Publications.
Petros G. Doukas, 2004, *Economic Theories, Principles of Management & Ancient Greek Thought*, Knowsys.
Plato, 1993, *Phaedon*, Cactus.
Plato, 2003, *The Apology of Socrates*, Zitros.
Plato, 2004, *Symposium 1 & 2 Volumes*, Zitros.
Stephen R. Covey, 2000, *The 7 Habits of Extremely Effective People*, Klitharithmos.
Stephen R. Covey, 2006, *The 8th Habit*, Klitharithmos.
Vassilis Kalfas, 2015, *Aristotle, Behind the Philosopher*, Kathimerini.

In French

Catherine Cudicio, 1999, *Maitriser l'art de la PNL*, Editions D'organisation.
Jacqueline de Romilly, 2012, *Ce que je crois*, de Fallois.

ABOUT THE AUTHOR

Barbara Asimakopoulou is an award-winning, international coach empowering leaders to develop their internal and external leadership skills for over two decades. She curates and provides applicable models and techniques that help organisations, executives, and professionals to evolve, understand, and fulfill their goals that lead to sustainability, work harmony, and personal well-being.

As the founder of *Human Resources Expertise*, an innovative company in the range of HRM services—Consulting, Training, & Coaching—Barbara Asimakopoulou has collaborated with some of the most prestigious global businesses.

She was awarded for her work in leadership skills development and cultural transformation.

Continuously pursuing lifelong education, Barbara holds the esteemed Professional Certified Coach credential from the International Coaching Federation (ICF), along with certifications from renowned worldwide coaching and leadership thinkers and institutions such as Marshall Goldsmith, Dave Drake, Peter Hawkins & David Clutterbuck, City University of London, and Coach University. Additionally, she holds a Master's Degree in Business Administration and a degree in chemistry.

Barbara's partnership with the National Kapodistrian University of Athens has led to the development of the e-learning educational program "Coaching Leadership: In the Footsteps of Socrates." Furthermore, she has successfully implemented the ICF-accredited coaching education program "Coaching Skills & Tools in Practice," which she co-designed with an international scientific council of experts, receiving excellent feedback.

With a wealth of experience in nurturing competent coaches and empowering leaders within various professional and community settings, Barbara draws upon her Greek heritage to unearth profound inspiration from classical philosophy. Her ultimate aspiration revolves around forging a harmonious connection between philosophical wisdom and the intricacies of daily existence, seamlessly integrating practical applications that pave the path towards a more enriched and joyous life.

Barbara is an accomplished keynote speaker and a published author. Among her other books are "The art of peace in the workplace" & "The Coach's Journal – Self Reflections."

In addition to writing, delivering lectures, and leading voluntary social movements, Barbara is driven by a clear and unwavering purpose: to assist modern individuals in finding their personal purpose, the path

ABOUT THE AUTHOR

that illuminates their existence, enabling self-realisation and inner emancipation. Ultimately, her mission is to empower individuals to become happier and more impactful leaders from within.

https://www.barbaraasimakopoulou.com/

PERSONAL LETTER

For those of you who have just read the book. Thank you.

The end of every journey is the beginning of a new one.

If you enjoyed this journey, how about the next one?

Do not wait until you stumble upon this book again in 5–10 years to remember all the essential insights you gained from it. Take the second most pivotal step that will forever transform your life.

The second step, I believe, involves acquiring a coaching education from a trustworthy institution that guarantees:

1. Personal growth and progress.
2. Enhanced leadership competencies.
3. Professional opportunities in a global environment.
4. A classical philosophy-based approach.

If this feels aligned, then I encourage you to enrol in "**Coaching Skills & Tools in Practice**."

This 10-month hybrid program offers English-speaking individuals as well as Greeks, the opportunity to obtain an internationally recognised professional certification, accredited by the esteemed International Coaching Federation.

We integrate teachings from classical sources and embrace the future of coaching by incorporating cutting-edge technology, artificial intelligence, and scientific disciplines such as neuroscience, leadership, management, mindfulness, art and positive psychology.

The program combines a unique four-day retreat that includes an immersion in classical teachings at their birthplace—Athens, Greece—and how they are incorporated into modern coaching. Prepared to be inspired by the wisdom of Plato, Socrates, Aristotle, and the Stoics.

Furthermore, the program offers you the chance to:

- practice and continuously improve with the guidance of experienced mentor coaches
- gain valuable coaching experience and establish yourself as a seasoned professional
- join a remarkable community of V.I.P.-Visionary, Innovative & Powerful coaches and leaders who will provide support, keep you informed, inspire your vision, and invigorate you to actively contribute to a sustainable and ethical society.

I firmly believe in your potential and in the brighter future that awaits you.

—Barbara Asimakopoulou
Your coach

PERSONAL LETTER

Go to www.BarbaraAsimakopoulou.com for more information, or message me at ba@hre.gr to book an appointment, and to help you decide what is best for you now.

To continue the journey, you can follow my accounts on Facebook, Instagram, and LinkedIn @Barbara Asimakopoulou.

Notes

Milton Keynes UK
Ingram Content Group UK Ltd.
UKHW050240100224
437572UK00001B/18